ESSENTIAL
Serger
REFERENCE TOOL

YOUR QUICK AND EASY VISUAL GUIDE

to Tension, Threading, Stitches, Seam Treatments
for Different Fabrics & Troubleshooting

KATRINA WALKER

C&T PUBLISHING
Another Maker Inspired!

Text copyright © 2024 by Katrina Walker

Photography and artwork copyright © 2024 by C&T Publishing, Inc.

Publisher: Amy Barrett-Daffin

Creative Director: Gailen Runge

Senior Editor: Roxane Cerda

Editor: Kathryn Patterson and Gailen Runge

Technical Editor: Julie Waldman

Cover/Book Designer: April Mostek

Production Coordinator: Zinnia Heinzmann

Illustrator: Aliza Shalit

Photography Coordinator: Rachel Ackley

Photography Assistant: Kaeley Hammond

Photography by Estefany Gonzalez for C&T Publishing, Inc., unless otherwise noted

Published by C&T Publishing, Inc., P.O. Box 1456, Lafayette, CA 94549

Attention Teachers: C&T Publishing, Inc., encourages the use of our books as texts for teaching. You can find lesson plans for many of our titles at ctpub.com or contact us at ctinfo@ctpub.com.

We take great care to ensure that the information included in our products is accurate and presented in good faith, but no warranty is provided, nor are results guaranteed. Having no control over the choices of materials or procedures used, neither the author nor C&T Publishing, Inc., shall have any liability to any person or entity with respect to any loss or damage caused directly or indirectly by the information contained in this book. For your convenience, we post an up-to-date listing of corrections on our website (ctpub.com). If a correction is not already noted, please contact our customer service department at ctinfo@ctpub.com or P.O. Box 1456, Lafayette, CA 94549.

Library of Congress Cataloging-in-Publication Data

Names: Walker, Katrina Ann, 1972- author.

Title: Essential serger reference tool : your quick and easy visual guide to tension, threading, stitches, seam treatments for different fabrics & troubleshooting / Katrina Walker.

Description: Lafayette, CA : C&T Publishing, [2024] | Summary: "Serge confidently with this pocket-sized guide! This book is jam-packed with techniques and troubleshooting charts for stress-free serging. Learn how to thread your serger, choose and use serger stitches, and serge different types of fabric. Build your skills with information on differential feed, securing seams, serging challenging shapes, and more"-- Provided by publisher.

Identifiers: LCCN 2023058900 | ISBN 9781644034231 (trade paperback) | ISBN 9781644034248 (ebook)

Subjects: LCSH: Serging--Handbooks, manuals, etc. | BISAC: CRAFTS & HOBBIES / Sewing | LCGFT: Handbooks and manuals.

Classification: LCC TT713 .W35 2024 | DDC 646.2/044--dc23/eng/20240202

LC record available at https://lccn.loc.gov/2023058900

Printed in China

10 9 8 7 6 5 4 3 2 1

ACKNOWLEDGMENTS

I would like to thank the following:

The C&T family for giving me the opportunity to write this book. I am thrilled to help sewing enthusiasts learn to love their sergers.

SVP Worldwide for providing me with their fabulous sergers. Being an educator for HUSQVARNA VIKING and PFAFF as well as a PFAFF brand ambassador is an honor and an amazing experience.

Sulky of America for generously supplying their fantastic threads and stabilizers.

Clover USA for supplying their truly wonderful Wonder Clips, pins, and other great tools and notions.

Vanessa Dyson for suggesting that I tackle this book in the first place, and for her continuing support and encouragement.

My mother, Kathy Bohnet, for purchasing "my" first serger. (Little did you know where that adventure would lead!) Thanks for allowing me to use your sewing tools and many, many yards of fabric.

Gail Brown, Cindy Cummins, Pati Palmer, Nancy Zieman, and other authors I studied when I was learning to use a serger all those years ago. Thank you for sharing your knowledge.

My student friends for your constant enthusiasm and inspiration. You always motivate me to work harder and to find better ways to make your sewing joyful.

Finally, and most importantly, my husband, Scott, who makes all of this possible by being the rock I lean upon. Thank you for your tremendous patience during this process and keeping the critters and me fed.

Contents

SERGER BASICS   8

Chapter 1: Get to Know Your Serger   9

Chapter 2: Threading Your Serger   25

Chapter 3: Choosing Serger Stitches   54

SERGER SKILL BUILDING   70

Chapter 4: Serging with Confidence   71

SERGER SPECIALTY STITCHES   87

Chapter 5: Flatlocking   88

Chapter 6: Rolled Hems   94

Chapter 7: Safety Stitch and Coverstitching   100

SERGER CONSTRUCTION TECHNIQUES   110

Chapter 8: Knit Construction Techniques   111

Chapter 9: Woven Construction Techniques   120

SPECIALTY TECHNIQUES AND TOOLS   126

Chapter 10: Serging Sheers and Delicates   127

Chapter 11: Specialty Tools   133

INDEX   140

ABOUT THE AUTHOR   143

BUILDING SKILLS

Here's what you'll learn in the five sections of this tool:

Serger Basics   8

  What a serger is and how it works

  Threading a serger with ease

  Creating balanced stitches and troubleshooting stitch issues

  Understanding serger stitches and their uses

Serger Skill Building   70

  Allowing for seam allowances and raw edges

  Discovering differential feed and its uses

  Starting and stopping serged seams

  Serging smooth curves and crisp corners

  Securing serged seams

Serger Specialty Stitches   87

  Featuring the flatlock for both function and fashion

  Using rolled hems for beautiful finishes, decorative effects, and more

  Safety stitching and coverstitching professional-looking seams and hems

Serger Construction Techniques   110

  Strategies for serging knit and woven fabrics

  Determining the best serger stitch for your seam

  Preparing seams for accurate serging

  Flat construction for fast, easy garment sewing

Specialty Techniques and Tools   126

  Serging delicate and sheer fabrics beautifully

  Embellishing with trims for fancy effects

  Utilizing optional serger accessories

EXPANDING YOUR KNOWLEDGE

Serger Basics

Is a Coverstitch Machine the same as a Serger?   10

Serger Needles Are Unique   15

Considerations When Purchasing a Serger   24

What Is Serger Thread?   25

Color-Coded Threading   26

Using The 2-Thread Converter   31

Rethreading Your Serger   38

Coverstitch-Capable Versus Coverstitch: What Are The Differences?   39

Threading Decorative Threads   51

As You Serge, So Shall You Rip   66

Serger Skill Building

What Are Serger Stitch Widths?   72

Serging Curves With Seam Allowances   78

Why Use the Cutting Blade?   79

Serger Specialty Stitches

Flatlock Topstitching   90

How Much Coverage?   96

Serger Construction Techniques

3-Thread Or 4-Thread?   113

Always Fit First   115

To Flatten Or Not To Flatten?   119

Bulk Can Be Beautiful   122

Interpreting Garment Patterns For Serging   122

Special Techniques and Tools

Stiffen For Success   128

EASY REFERENCE

Facts at your fingertips with detailed charts:

Troubleshooting Serger Stitches   52

Selecting Serger Stitches for Knits and Strech Fabrics   67

Selecting Serger Stitches for Woven Fabrics   68

TIPS FOR SUCCESS

Serger Basics

How Many Threads Do I Need? 10

Love Your Manual 11

Discount Store Pros and Cons 24

Tweezers Are a Must! 30

No Shortcuts! 38

Create a Serger Reference Notebook 55

Nearly Invisible Hems 58

Beautiful Braids 59

Fancy Tucks 60

Oh, Baby! 61

Right Side Up 63

Serger Skill Building

Make A Seam Allowance Stitching Guide 73

Pinning for Serging 74

No Glue Zone 74

Helping Hands 76

Need a Lift? 77

Slow It Down! 78

The Handwheel Is Handy 82

Serger Specialty Stitches

Test First! 91

No Tug of War! 97

More Thread, Please! 98

No Whiskers! 99

When in Doubt, Rethread 103

Stick That Hem 106

Save Scraps—Use Stabilizer! 106

The Manual Is Always Right 109

Serger Construction Techniques

Test, Test, Test! 112

Taming Tricky Knits 113

Distorted by Design 114

Flatlock for Wovens 121

Whisker-Free Zone 123

Practical Skill Building 123

Always Fit First 125

Sew Twice, Cut Once 125

Fancy Footwork 125

Special Techniques and Tools

Stop the Slippage 130

Easy Lace Alignment 131

Serger
Basics

Your Serger

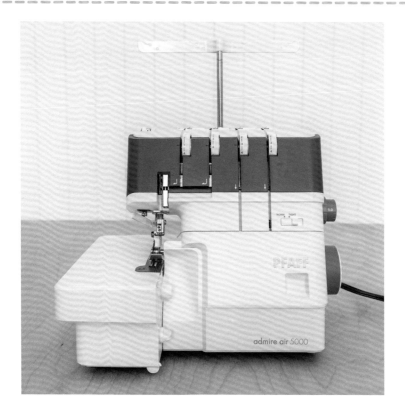

WHAT IS A SERGER?

Is a serger a sewing machine? The answer is yes—and no. Like
a sewing machine, a serger (also called an *overlock* or *merrow
machine*) uses threads to stitch a seam. But unlike a traditional
sewing machine, a serger uses a set of loopers rather than a
bobbin to catch the needle threads and create a stitch. This
seam is designed to interlock over the edge of the fabric, which
has the benefit of finishing the seam edge in the same operation
as stitching the seam, thus *overlocking* the seam. A serged seam

has many advantages over a traditional lockstitched seam, being stronger and more elastic, and a serger generally sews faster than a lockstitch sewing machine. A serger does have a few limitations, which means it does not entirely replace a traditional sewing machine. However, its advantages make it the perfect companion to your sewing machine and a must-have for any sewing enthusiast.

Sergers use multiple threads that can form a variety of stitches. The actual number of threads used varies depending on the stitch created. A basic serger may use 2–4 threads, whereas a serger that is also able to create chain stitches and coverstitch hems uses at least 5 threads. Some sergers can create decorative stitch techniques that use up to 10 threads!

Tip // How Many Threads Do I Need?
The ability to convert to 2 threads is handy, and 5-thread specialty stitches are great. But if your serger doesn't have these abilities don't worry—the majority of serger work is performed with 3–4 threads.

THE BASIC PARTS OF A SERGER

Although each brand and model of serger may be slightly different, there are basic parts that are common to all sergers.

Is a Coverstitch Machine the same as a Serger?

A close relation to the serger is the *coverstitch machine*. This cousin of the serger performs only the chain stitch and coverstitches, which look like a traditional straight stitch on the upper side of the fabric and like a chain or an overlock stitch underneath. The chain stitch can be used for seaming, but it can be more easily undone than serger or sewing machine seams, so it is best used for basting or reinforcement. A coverstitch is primarily used for hemming fabrics, particularly knits, but can also be used to attach binding, to create belt loops, to sew decorative effects, and for other specialty items. A coverstitch machine cannot create an overlock seam, so consider it an accessory machine and not a substitute for a serger or overlock machine.

Tip // Love Your Manual

The serger manual is your most important tool. It contains information about the location of your serger's parts, as well as detailed threading diagrams and instructions. Keep it near your serger for quick reference.

Let's look at a basic serger and identify the parts in sequence as if we are going to thread it. Although every serger model has its unique characteristics, most parts and features are universal. Be sure to reference your serger's manual to check the location of your particular serger's functions and features.

One obvious difference between a serger and a traditional sewing machine is the thread cone rack.

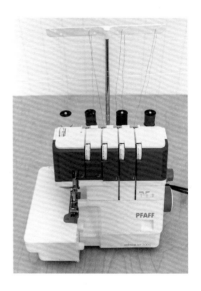

Because sergers do not use a bobbin, they can use thread much more efficiently. Specialty serger thread is sold in cones to make feeding large quantities of thread easier. The thread stand helps to keep threads untangled as they feed into the thread guides and tension discs.

The thread guides ensure the thread moves smoothly through the thread path to and from the tension discs. The tension discs work the same for a serger as the tension discs on a traditional sewing machine. Thread passes between a set of discs, which squeeze in on either side of the thread to create a certain amount of drag or tension on the thread necessary to create correct stitch formation.

Thread guides and tension discs with color coding

The amount of tension needed varies depending on the type of stitch used and sometimes on the thickness of the fabric. Some computerized serger tension discs automatically adjust depending on the stitch selected, and others are manually adjusted. Computerized sergers with automatic tension discs usually still offer the ability to manually adjust the tension to fine-tune the serger stitch performance. From the tension discs, the threads then travel along additional thread paths to the loopers and needles. The loopers are threaded before the needles.

If we open up the front of the serger, we can see the threads travel from the tension discs along thread guides, creating the thread paths for the loopers.

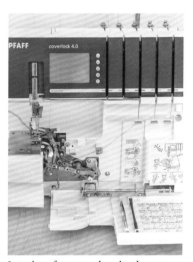

Interior of serger, showing loopers and looper thread path with numbers

If your serger uses an air system to blow the looper threads through the thread guides, you may not see the actual thread paths due to the enclosed nature of the air system. Instead, you will see the small ports where the looper threads will be inserted.

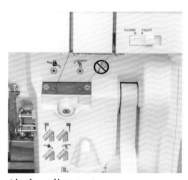

Air-threading ports

Air-threading sergers generally also have a selector lever for directing which looper port will be threaded and a second lever or a button to activate the air-threading function.

Air-threading lever and selector

The loopers are the most essential components of your serger, and they are what work together to create an overlock (or cover) stitch. All sergers have an upper and lower looper.

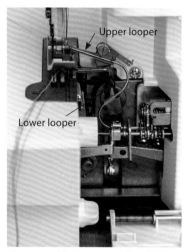

Upper looper

Lower looper

Close-up of looper area, showing upper and lower loopers

Sergers that can create a chain stitch or coverstitch will have a third looper as well. It is important to identify and locate the placement of each looper, because these loopers must be threaded in a particular order for overlock stitches to form properly.

Chain-stitch looper

Close-up of chain-stitch looper

Some sergers also have a 2-thread converter on the upper looper that allows an overlock stitch to be formed using 2 threads instead of 3.

Close-up of 2-thread converter

The needles are threaded after the loopers. Just as with the looper threads, there are designated thread paths and guides leading from the tension discs to the needles.

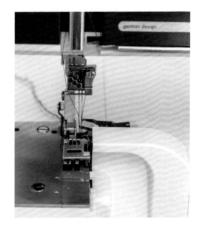

Another difference between sergers and traditional sewing machines is the needle clamp, or needle holder. Sergers use a variety of needle positions depending on the stitch used and number of threads. Most

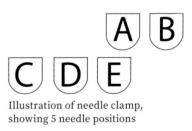

Illustration of needle clamp, showing 5 needle positions

sergers will have at least a left and right needle position. These are used for overlock stitches using either a left needle for wider 2- or 3-thread stitches, a right needle for narrow 2- or 3-thread stitches, or both needles for a 4-thread overlock. Coverstitch-capable sergers will additionally have up to 3 coverstitch needle positions depending on the model of machine. These are usually positioned forward and to the left of the standard overlock needle positions in the needle clamp. When a stitch is selected, it is important to note of the location of each needle position for correct stitch formation.

Serger Needles Are Unique

There are two differences to note between serger needles and sewing machine needles. First, serger needles are not the same as traditional sewing needles. Serger needles are marked as "overlock" or by their type designation, usually ELx705, although some sergers do use regular sewing machine needles. Be sure to read your manual!

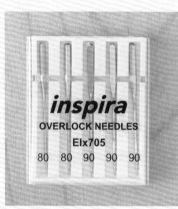

Overlock needles

Second, serger needles are offset when they are inserted correctly. If you have a left and right needle, such as for a 4-thread overlock stitch, the left needle will be lower than the right needle.

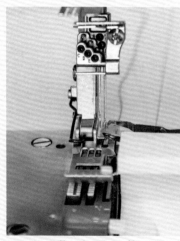

Serger needles showing offset points

Sergers have a handwheel just like a traditional sewing machine. The handwheel can be turned to move parts for easier threading or to manually form a stitch. Refer to your machine's manual to see which direction the wheel should be turned.

The stitching area has several specialized parts. Some might be familiar, like the feed dogs and the sewing foot.

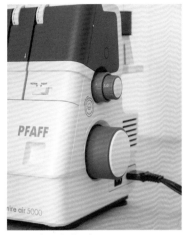

Serger handwheel

Although a serger's presser foot looks a bit odd, it performs the same function as a presser foot on a traditional sewing machine. Most serging is done with a standard foot, but there are various specialty feet available for most brands. These specialty feet make it easy to create many different techniques, from beading to belt loops, depending on the functionality of your particular serger. Your serger manual should list any specialty feet available for your serger and how to change the feet.

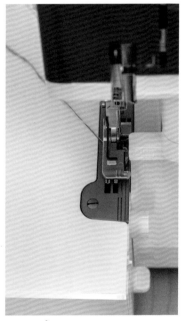

Presser foot

Tip // Fancy Feet
Explore serger specialty feet in Chapter 11: Specialty Tools (page 133).

The serger foot is lifted by a presser foot lifter, which may be a lever on the back of the serger, or a knob or lever on the side of the serger.

Presser foot lifter

Sergers also have a presser foot pressure-adjustment knob. The standard setting is fine for most fabrics, but very thick or thin fabrics may not feed correctly when serging with standard pressure. Adjusting the presser foot pressure can solve this problem.

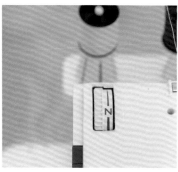

Presser foot pressure adjustment

Under the serger presser foot, on the bed of the serger, is the stitch plate. This large metal plate has openings for the feed dogs, plus it contains parts that help the needles and loopers to form stitches. Some sergers use multiple removable stitch plates to perform different functions, whereas others use just 1 standard plate with movable parts.

Stitch plate area with feed dogs, stitch needles and finger, and cutting blade

Unlike a traditional sewing machine that features 1 set of feed dogs under the sewing foot, most sergers have 2 large sets, one in front of the other. Having a longer set of feed dogs allows fabric to be fed more effectively through the serger. The 2 sets of feed dogs also allow what is called *differential feed*. Differential feed is a feature that allows the front feed dogs to move at a variable rate, so that it

Feed dogs

feeds fabric into the serger either slower, the same speed, or faster than the back feed dogs. This allows knit fabrics to feed through the serger without stretching out and delicate fabrics to serge without puckering. It also makes it possible to create decorative effects.

In the stitch-forming area of the serger stitch plate are a set of needles pointing to the back of the serger (1). The serger uses these needles, and a stitch "finger" (2) to form the seam with interlocking loops and ensure that the seam created is a particular width. If the stitch finger is removed, a very narrow stitch is formed. Many sergers use a sliding lever (3) to move the stitch finger into or out of the stitching area. Other

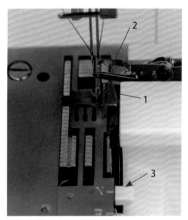

Stitch forming area

sergers use a completely different stitch plate from the standard sewing plate.

Sergers also use cutting blades, located to the right of the stitch area, to trim the seam during sewing. The cut is performed using a stationary blade and a movable blade.

Cutting blades

For some stitches, the upper cutting blade is disengaged or otherwise moved so that the fabric is not trimmed during stitching. The upper cutting blade is designed to be able to drop down out of the stitching area. Some sergers simply use a large nut that is part of the blade attachment that can be pulled and turned. Others use a lever to move the blade. Consult your serger manual for the correct method for your particular serger.

Upper cutting-blade adjustment nut

On many machines, the cutting blades can be adjusted to cut the seam allowance in variable widths, ensuring the seam is the correct width for the overlock stitch to form properly. These adjustments are performed using the blade adjustment knob.

Blade cutting–width adjustment knob

Other serger components are used to select stitches and control serging speed. These features will vary depending on whether or not your serger is computerized and how many customizing options are available.

If your serger is solely mechanical, all of the information for setting up the various stitches for your serger will be located in your serger manual. If your serger is computerized, much of this information may be available on your serger's screen interface.

The screen interface is an obvious feature of a computerized serger. This screen might have touch capability, or it may display various options based on hard buttons located beside the screen. Self-tensioning

Computerized serger screen

computerized sergers will often show stitch selections on the screen that will then set up the tension discs for the amount of tension thought optimal to form the selected stitch.

Unfortunately, automatic stitch selection does not necessarily mean that the physical components such as needles, cutting blades, loopers, and other functions are automatically changed as well. But computerized sergers will

Automatic stitch selection

often show on the screen which of these need to be either used or disengaged in order to form the stitch, which is very handy.

Many computerized sergers also offer the option of customizing serger stitch settings. Some will allow the customized setting to be saved for future use. Although automatic tensioning works well, there are many variables in serging, such as fabric thickness or thread types. You may also want to intentionally

Computerized serger screen showing recommended settings

alter the stitch setting to achieve a decorative effect.

Sergers sew at a very fast speed. Thankfully, sergers commonly offer an adjustable speed function that limits the top stitching speed. This function might be accessed using a mechanical slider, buttons, or touch screen icons, depending on your serger.

Speed adjustment slider
Photo by Katrina Walker

Of course, the main speed control for your serger, just as with a traditional sewing machine, is your foot control. Some are more sensitive than others; use the foot control along with the speed adjustment to fine-tune your serger so it operates at a comfortable speed.

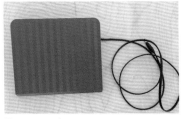

Foot control

Finally, the most important feature you need to find on your serger—the power-cord interface and on/off switch. It would be impossible to serge without these essentials! Thankfully they are also universal to both sewing machines and sergers. Consult your manual if you are unable to find your power switch or cord interface.

Power cord interface / power switch

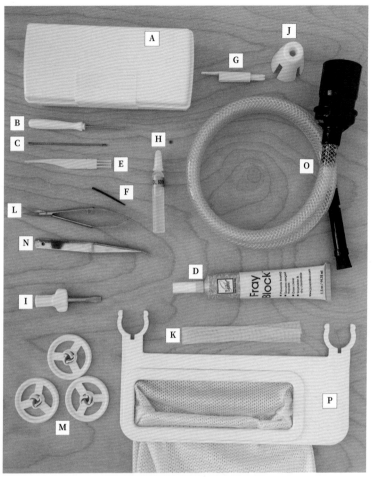

Accessory tools

There are several tools that will make using your serger easier. Some of them likely came with your serger, and others will need to be purchased separately.

A. Accessory box This box, usually included with your serger, contains the most essential tools for operating your machine. If you do not have one, create one of your own to keep your tools handy.

B. Allen wrench Changing the needles and needle positions on your serger requires the use of a small Allen wrench.

C. Double-ended needle A double-ended needle, bodkin, or similar tool is handy for pulling thread tails back through the seam to secure them.

D. Fray inhibitor This is a liquid that keeps threads and fabrics from fraying. It is useful for sealing the ends of seams so that the thread chains can be cut neatly.

E. Lint brush Sergers generate a lot of lint as well as bits and pieces of fabric. A small lint brush is essential for helping to keep your serger clean.

F. Looper threader Some specialty threads are challenging to pull through the loopers when threading the serger. Looper threaders can help with this.

G. Needle threader A needle threader is always handy for challenging threads.

H. Sewing machine oil Sergers have many moving parts, and some of them need to be oiled regularly, according to your manual's instructions.

I. Screwdriver Cutting blades and other parts of the serger need a screwdriver to change or modify.

J. Thread cone holders These slide onto the thread pins to keep thread cones steady during use.

K. Thread nets Some threads, such as metallics, benefit from the use of a thread net to keep the threads from being tangled as they feed quickly from the spool.

L. Thread snips A sharp pair of thread snips is handy for neatly trimming thread chains after sealing.

M. Thread unreeling discs These plastic discs are placed on top of traditional sewing thread spools to help them to release thread smoothly and quickly.

N. Tweezers Tweezers are essential to ease the pulling of thread through guides and needles.

O. Vacuum attachment A generic vacuum attachment with extra small tips and brushes is perfect for cleaning out sergers.

P. Waste catcher This is essential for keeping your work area clean. Your waste catcher can be a commercially made serger waste tray or simply a small bag taped to the front of your serger.

Considerations When Purchasing a Serger

Many sewing enthusiasts recognize that a serger is a great tool to add to their sewing equipment. But which one? There are many choices to consider, not only of brands but also of serger features. The main factors to bear in mind are number of threads (which determines the number of stitches the serger can perform), ease of threading, and dealer support.

Before shopping for a serger, it's helpful to consider how it will be used. Do you plan to mostly use it to finish seam allowances for sewing projects, basic sewing, or the occasional rolled hem? If so, then a basic 2-3-4 thread serger will likely meet your needs. If you plan on creating heavy duty garments that need a safety stitch or producing professional-looking sportswear with stretch fabrics, you will want a 5-thread serger. Some sergers have specialty feet and accessories available as well. These make it easy to create blind hems, to add elastic while serging, or even to attach beads or lace to create fancy edgings. Ask about available accessories.

Once you know what type of serger you want, ease of use is your next consideration. It's best to buy your serger from a sewing machine dealership where you can sit down and try the serger with a variety of fabrics before buying. If the serger is easy to thread and simple to operate, you are more likely to use it.

Finally, consider the quality of support available. Ideally, the sewing machine dealer will offer training for you to learn to use your machine. They may even have ongoing classes for serger users. A reliable repair service is also handy to have for maintenance and in case of problems. All of these factors can greatly improve and enhance your experience as a serger owner.

Tip // Discount Store Pros and Cons
Buying a serger from a large home goods store may be the cheapest option. But user support for these purchases is limited and inexpensive sergers can be more difficult to use, produce poor results, and have a shorter useful life.

CHAPTER 2

Threading Your Serger

Threading a serger is intimidating to many sewing enthusiasts. Multiple threads, loopers, and moving parts can make threading seem complicated and frightening. With a bit of practice, threading your serger will be simple!

What Is Serger Thread?

Serger or overlocking thread is sold on cones to make it easier to feed quickly through your serger as well as more cost effective, since there is more thread on a cone than a spool. Although this is specifically designed for serger use, it is not the only compatible thread.

Serging can be done using a wide variety of threads. Decorative threads such as those used for machine embroidery, textured nylon, serger "yarn," and even metallics can be used in a serger. Most of these add to the appearance of the serged seam or hem, but some of them, especially the textured or "wooly" nylon, can be used to enhance seam performance.

Specialty threads are normally only used in the loopers. Loopers have the advantage of larger thread eyes, which make them more forgiving to larger or more delicate threads. Looper threads are caught by the needle(s) but do not actually pass through the fabric.

The most important thing to understand about threading sergers is that unlike a traditional sewing machine, sergers are threaded in a particular order. An overlocked seam is created using multiple threads to form interlocking loops, more like knitting than a regular sewing machine lockstitch. If the loopers and needles are threaded out of order, the stitch cannot form. Many air-threading sergers can be threaded in random order, but they are the exception.

Serger threaded with color-coded thread

Photo by Katrina Walker

Some sergers require that the serger be set into threading mode, through the use of a lever, switch, or handwheel position. If your serger requires this (check your manual for specifics), be sure to set the serger for threading mode before threading.

Serger manuals often use color-coded diagrams to illustrate the threading path for the serger. Often these diagrams are also printed on the inside of the looper cover for quick reference.

Sample threading diagram showing colors

Color-Coded Threading

Serger threading diagrams are color coded to make it easier to see the individual threading paths for each looper and needle. When you are learning to thread your serger and to create the various serger stitches, it is very helpful to thread your serger with colors matching those on the diagram. This makes it much easier to see if your thread path matches that of your manual diagram. Plus, it will help to diagnose any thread tension issues when creating stitches.

THREADING FOR OVERLOCK STITCHES

All sergers are able to create an overlock stitch using at least 3 threads. These 3 threads consist of the upper looper, the lower looper, and a needle. There are a variety of stitches that can be made using these 3 threads, created by adjusting the thread tension, the stitch finger placement, and the needle widths. Most sergers also have the capability of using 4 threads by incorporating a second needle, to create a "safety" overlock stitch with greater strength. Whether using 3 threads or 4 threads, the initial threading process is the same.

Opening the Tension Discs

Before starting to thread any component of the serger, first open the thread tension discs. This is done by either turning a dial, raising the presser foot, or pressing a button. Check your serger manual to determine the correct procedure for your model. The tension discs need to be open while threading to ensure that the thread passes through the discs properly. If the discs are closed, the thread might lay on top of the discs, which prevents thread tension from occurring. Incorrect thread tension causes poor stitch quality and prevents specialty stitches from forming correctly.

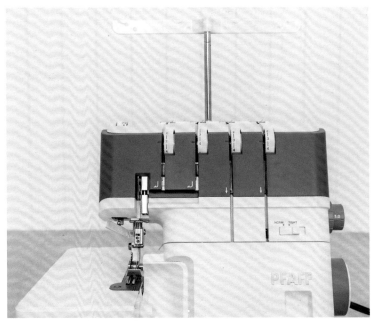

Thread tension discs or dials

Threading the Loopers

When threading a serger, the loopers are threaded first—*before* the needles.

In the case of an air-threading serger, the air-threading system may thread only the lower looper. Some air-threading systems will thread both the upper and lower looper. It is important to check the serger manual to determine which loopers are air threaded and whether the loopers need to be threaded in a particular order.

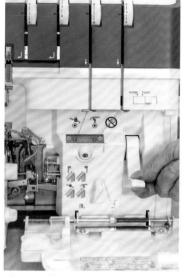

Air-threading serger looper air ports

Air-threading sergers use a set of threading ports for introducing thread into the looper air system. A selector lever may be used to determine which looper port is activated when the air-system button or lever is pressed.

THREADING THE UPPER LOOPER

Traditional sergers (those that do not use air-threading systems) generally start threading with the upper looper. To begin threading the upper looper, first open the thread tension discs and pull the thread through any upper threading guides. This portion of the threading process is basically the same for all loopers.

Upper looper

After the upper thread guides and tension discs are threaded, the upper looper thread path enters a set of unique thread guides specific to threading the upper looper. These are typically shown using a color-coded threading diagram.

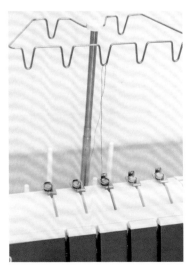

Threading through tension discs and upper guides with upper looper thread

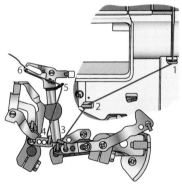

Typical upper looper threading path

Follow the color-coded threading path, paying careful attention to the location of all thread guides.

TIP // Tweezers Are a Must!
Use your long, narrow curve-tipped serger tweezers to help pull the thread through any thread guides in tight spaces. They make threading much easier.

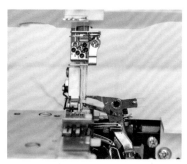

Close-up of upper looper with looper eye threaded

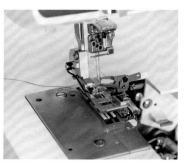

Pull thread from upper looper to back of stitch plate.

Once you pull the thread through the upper looper thread guides, you will thread the upper looper itself. Using your tweezers, thread the looper eye from front to back. Be sure to pull through at least 4″ (10.2cm) of thread.

Place the upper looper thread to the back of the stitch plate, making sure there is enough thread length to easily grasp the end of the thread tail behind the serger presser foot.

Using The 2-Thread Converter

Some overlock stitches use a special converter mechanism on the upper looper to form stitches using only the lower looper. For these stitches, the mechanism is engaged by inserting it into the eye of the upper looper, and only the lower looper is threaded.

2 Thread Converter
Open/Disengaged

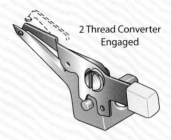

2 Thread Converter
Engaged

THREADING THE LOWER LOOPER

Lower looper

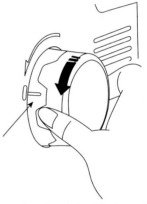

Mark on handwheel for lower looper threading position

Once the upper looper has been threaded, it is time to thread the lower looper. The lower looper is less accessible than the upper looper for threading. As a result, different models of serger will use varying methods to make threading the lower looper easier.

When threading the lower looper, the handwheel is turned to move the looper into the optimal position for threading. Some sergers have a mark on the handwheel that is aligned by turning the handwheel toward yourself. Others may recommend simply turning the handwheel toward you until the looper moves into position as indicated by its spacing from the stitch plate edge. Check your manual for your serger's specific recommendations.

As with the upper loopers, the lower looper thread must first be threaded through the upper thread guides and tension discs. Make sure the tension discs are open during threading.

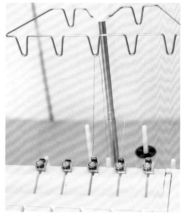

Threading through tension discs and upper guides with lower looper thread

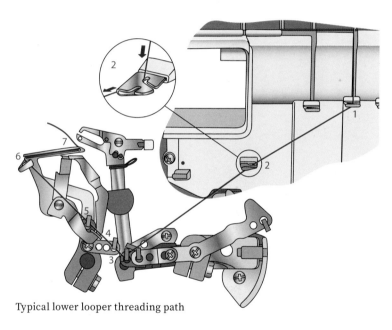

Typical lower looper threading path

Once the upper thread guides and tension discs are threaded, the lower looper thread path enters its own set of unique thread guides. As with the upper loopers, the lower looper threading path is typically illustrated with a color-coded threading diagram. Follow the color-coded threading path, paying careful attention to the location of all thread guides.

Threading lever for lower looper

Close-up of lower looper with looper eye threaded

Threading the lower looper eye is more challenging than the upper looper, because the thread must first catch onto the back of the lower looper. This portion of the lower looper is often hidden within the serger cover, and so various mechanical methods are used to push the thread into place. This may be a push rod, a threading lever, or similar device.

Thread the lower looper eye from front to back using your tweezers. Once the lower looper eye is threaded, use the threading lever or similar device to finish threading the lower looper. As always, check with your manual to ensure the correct procedure for your serger.

Place the lower looper thread to the back of the stitch plate in the same manner as the upper looper, making sure there is enough thread length to easily grasp the end of the thread tail behind the serger presser foot.

Pull thread from lower looper to back of stitch plate

Threading the Needles

Once the serger loopers are threaded, it is time to thread the needles. Sergers have a variety of needle positions available. There may be needle positions for both overlocking and coverstitching, depending on the serger. If there are coverstitch needle positions, they will be located forward and to the left of the overlocking needles. An overlocking-only serger will have 2 needle positions: left and right.

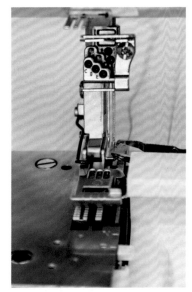

Close-up of needle bar

THREADING THE RIGHT NEEDLE

When threading a 3-thread overlock stitch, either the left or right needle may be used, depending on whether a wide or narrow stitch width is wanted. If threading for a 4-thread overlock stitch, 2 needles are used. In this instance, the right needle is typically threaded first (unless indicated otherwise by your serger manual). The right needle is used singly for creating narrow 3-thread overlock stitches.

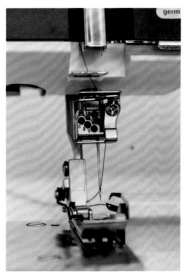

Needle bar with right needle in position

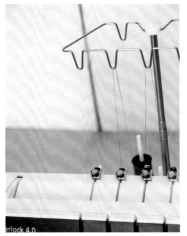

Threading through tension discs and upper guides with right needle thread

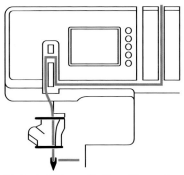

Typical right-needle threading path

To thread the right needle, begin with opening the tension discs and threading the right needle thread guides immediately before and after the tension discs.

As with the loopers, the right-needle threading path is usually indicated by a color-coded diagram. Be sure to follow the diagram carefully, as each needle thread typically has its own set of guides, especially in the area just above the needle.

Once the right-needle thread has been threaded through the guides, thread the needle from front to back, the same as for a traditional sewing machine. Pull at least 4″ (10.2cm) of thread through the needle and place it under the presser foot toward the back.

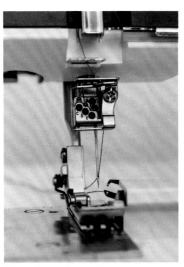

Threaded right needle

The left needle is used singly for wide 3-thread overlock stitches. If used on its own, it can be threaded immediately after the loopers. But if used with the right needle to create a 4-thread overlock stitch, it is usually threaded after the right needle.

Needle bar with left and right needles in position, with right needle threaded

To thread the left needle, begin with opening the tension discs and threading the guides immediately before and after the tension discs.

Threading through tension discs and upper guides with left-needle thread

Continue to thread the left needle by following the diagram in your serger manual. It is always important to follow the thread path carefully to ensure correct stitch formation.

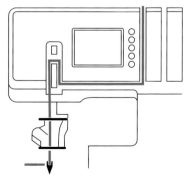

Typical left-needle threading path

Once the thread path has been completely threaded, thread the eye of the left needle from front to back. Pull at least 4″ (10.2cm) of thread through the needle and place it under the presser foot toward the back.

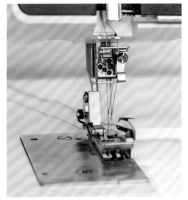

Threaded left needle

Starting the Overlock Stitch

The overlock stitch is started by creating a thread chain.

Once the loopers and needles are threaded, close the front cover and bring the thread tails across the stitch plate so that they are behind and slightly to the left of the presser foot. You may need to lift the presser foot to do this.

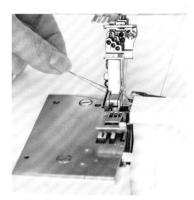

Grasp serger threads in left hand to left of presser foot.

As you hold the threads with your left hand, use your right hand to turn the handwheel toward you. Turn the handwheel several times, watching to see if an overlock chain is forming.

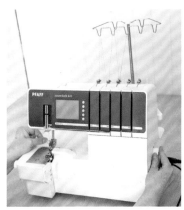

Hold serger chain with one hand and turn handwheel with the other.

If a chain is forming, gently press on the foot control while continuing to pull slightly (maintaining a light tension) on the thread. Create a thread chain at least 4″ (10.2cm) long. Stop serging, let go of the thread chain, and place a piece of scrap fabric under the presser foot. Serge a test sample, checking to see if the stitches are forming correctly. Serge off the edge of the fabric and continue to stitch for at least 5″ (12.7cm) as you gently pull the fabric toward the back of the serger, forming a long chain. Cut the thread chain, leaving at least 3″ (7.6cm) of chain in place on the serger.

Overlock thread chain   **Serge scrap of fabric to test stitches.**

TIP // No Shortcuts!
If your thread breaks or stitches are not forming, cut all of the threads and rethread in the proper sequence.

Rethreading Your Serger

If your thread breaks while serging, or if a thread chain is not forming, you need to rethread your serger. Just as with threading a serger, rethreading a serger needs to be done in the correct order:

1. Unthread the needle(s).

2. Unthread the loopers.

3. Thread the upper looper.

4. Thread the lower looper.

5. Thread the needles from right to left.

6. Start the overlock stitch by turning the handwheel toward you as you grasp and gently pull the threads to the back of the serger.

Coverstitch-Capable Versus Coverstitch: What Are The Differences?

Both coverstitch-capable sergers and coverstitch machines can sew a chain stitch and coverstitches. But a coverstitch machine cannot sew an overlock stitch or any of its variations.

So why own a coverstitch machine? It can be handy to have a separate machine set up just for coverstitching. Often coverstitch machines also offer free-arm capability, which makes it easier to sew hems and necklines.

If you own a coverstitch machine, be aware that the needles will likely be threaded in the reverse order (left to right) from your serger (right to left). As with any machine, it is important to check your user manual to ensure the correct settings.

Threading the Chain–Stitch Looper

Coverlock and chain-stitch–capable sergers have a third looper called the *chain-stitch looper*. This looper is used to form both chain stitches and coverstitches. This is a secondary lower looper, which may be used singly or in combination with the upper or lower looper, depending on the stitch used. If used together with the upper or lower looper, the chain-stitch looper is threaded last.

Chain-stitch looper

Turn handwheel counterclockwise.

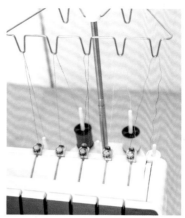

Threading through tension discs and upper guides with chain-stitch looper thread

The chain-stitch looper is located to the left of the lower looper, so it must be moved manually into position to thread. This usually requires turning the handwheel toward you until this looper moves into its furthest position to the right. Check your manual for your serger's specific recommendations.

As with the upper and lower loopers, the chain-stitch looper thread must first be threaded through the upper thread guides and tension discs. Make sure the tension discs are open during threading.

Once the upper thread guides and tension discs are threaded, the chain-stitch looper thread path enters its own set of unique thread guides. The chain-stitch threading path is illustrated with a color-coded threading diagram in the same way as the upper and lower loopers. Follow the color-coded threading path, paying careful attention to the location of all thread guides.

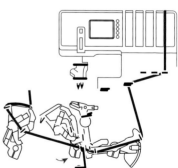

Typical chain-stitch looper threading path

Threading lever for chain-stitch looper

As with the lower looper, the thread must catch onto the back of the chain-stitch looper. This portion of the chain-stitch looper is often hidden within the serger cover, and so various mechanical methods are used to push the thread into place. This may be a push rod, threading lever, or similar device.

Close-up of chain-stitch looper with eye threaded

Thread the chain-stitch looper eye from front to back, using your tweezers. Then use the threading lever (or similar device) to finish threading the chain-stitch looper.

Place the chain-stitch looper thread to the back of the stitch plate in the same manner as the other looper threads, making sure there is enough thread length to easily grasp the end of the thread tail behind the serger presser foot.

Threading the Needles for Chain Stitch and Coverstitch

The chain-stitch and coverstitch functions use a set of needle holders that are located to the left of the overlock needle positions. Chain-stitch and coverstitch-capable sergers will generally have 3 of these needle positions: the right coverstitch needle, the middle coverstitch or chain-stitch needle, and the left coverstitch needle.

Needle bar for chain-stitch and coverstitch needles

THREADING THE CHAIN-STITCH NEEDLE

When stitching a chain stitch, only the middle coverstitch needle position is used. It is possible to sew a chain stitch combined with an overlock stitch; to do this, 1 or 2 needles in the overlock needle positions would also be used. In this instance, the overlock needles are threaded in the traditional order (from right to left) and then the chain-stitch needle is threaded.

Needle bar with chain-stitch needle in position

To thread the chain-stitch needle, begin with opening the tension discs for the thread path furthest to the left, and thread the needle thread guides immediately before and after the tension discs.

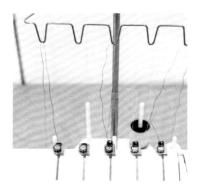

Threading through tension discs and upper guides with chain-stitch needle thread

Continue to follow the chain-stitch–needle threading path as indicated by the color-coded diagram in your manual. Be sure to pay special attention to the location of the guides and needle position in the area just above the needle.

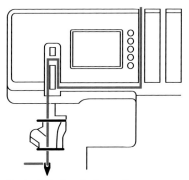

Typical chain-stitch needle threading path

Once the chain-stitch needle thread has been threaded through the guides, thread the needle from front to back. Pull at least 4″ (10.2cm) of thread through the needle and place it under the presser foot toward the back.

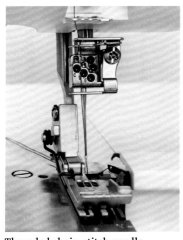

Threaded chain-stitch needle

A coverstitch can be serged using a set of either 2 or 3 needles, depending on whether a double or triple coverstitch is wanted. Like the overlock needles, these needles are threaded in order from the right to the left. Some sergers have 5 sets of needle positions and some use 4 to accommodate the various overlock and coverstitch types. Check with your serger manual and look closely at your needle bar to determine which set your coverstitch-capable serger uses.

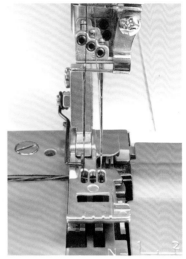

Needle bar with left and right coverstitch needles in position, with right needle threaded
Photo by Katrina Walker

To thread the right coverstitch needle, begin with opening the tension discs and threading the guides immediately before and after the tension discs.

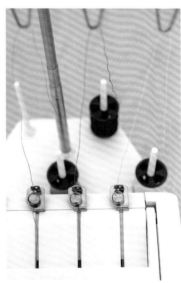

Threading through tension discs and upper guides with right coverstitch needle thread

Continue to thread the right coverstitch needle by following the diagram in your serger manual. It is always important to follow the thread path carefully to ensure correct stitch formation.

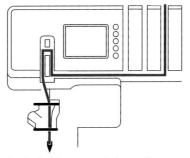

Typical right coverstitch needle threading path

Once the thread path has been completely threaded, thread the eye of the right coverstitch needle from front to back. Pull at least 4″ (10.2cm) of thread through the needle and place it under the presser foot toward the back.

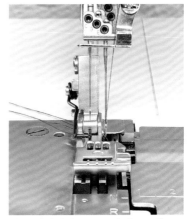

Threaded right coverstitch needle
Photo by Katrina Walker

THREADING THE MIDDLE COVERSTITCH NEEDLE

When a triple coverstitch or narrow double coverstitch is wanted, the middle coverstitch needle position is used. This is the same needle position as for the chain stitch, but a different tension disc (and therefore thread path) is used. The middle coverstitch needle is threaded after the right coverstitch needle, unless used for a narrow double coverstitch. In that case, the middle coverstitch needle is used instead of the right.

To thread the middle needle, begin with opening the tension discs and threading the guides immediately before and after the tension discs.

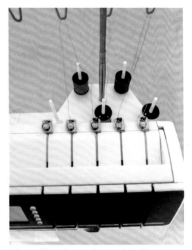

Threading through tension discs and upper guides with middle coverstitch needle thread

Continue to thread the middle needle by following the diagram in your serger manual. It is always important to follow the thread path carefully to ensure correct stitch formation.

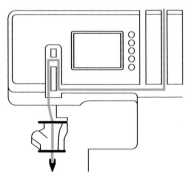

Typical middle coverstitch needle threading path

Once the thread path has been completely threaded, thread the eye of the middle coverstitch needle from front to back. Pull at least 4″ (10.2cm) of thread through the needle and place it under the presser foot toward the back.

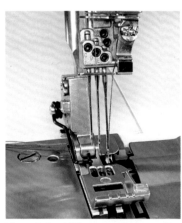

Threaded middle coverstitch needle
Photo by Katrina Walker

The left coverstitch needle is used to create both wide and narrow coverstitches. It is threaded last.

To thread the left coverstitch needle, begin with opening the tension discs and threading the guides immediately before and after the tension discs.

Threading through tension discs and upper guides with left coverstitch needle thread

Continue to thread the left coverstitch needle by following the diagram in your serger manual. It is always important to follow the thread path carefully to ensure correct stitch formation.

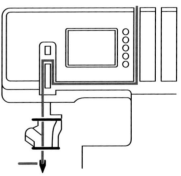

Typical left coverstitch needle threading path

Once the thread path has been completely threaded, thread the eye of the left coverstitch needle from front to back. Pull at least 4″ (10.2cm) of thread through the needle and place it under the presser foot toward the back.

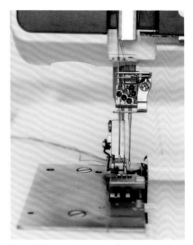

Needle bar with left and right coverstitch needles shown and threaded

Starting the Chain Stitch

Unlike overlock stitches, a chain stitch must be started with fabric under the needles.

To start the chain stitch after threading, place a piece of scrap fabric at least 4″ (10.2cm) long under the presser foot. Sew on the fabric. At the end of the fabric, pull it gently to the back of the machine and chain off.

Starting chain stitch in scrap fabric
Photo by Katrina Walker

Starting the Coverstitch

A coverstitch must be started with fabric under the needles.

To start a coverstitch after threading, place a piece of scrap fabric at least 3″ (7.6cm) long under the presser foot. Sew on the fabric to test the stitch until you reach the end of the fabric piece.

It is equally important that the coverstitch be well secured before removing from the serger. Coverstitches are very easy to unravel from the end of the seam. An excellent way to secure a coverstitch is by backstitching the end.

1. Stop just before sewing off the end of the fabric and release the needle thread tension by raising the presser foot.

2. Pull a small amount of slack in the needle threads so that the fabric can be released from the stitch fingers and the needles placed just behind the previous few stitches.

3. Coverstitch over the previous stitches to lock the coverstitching.

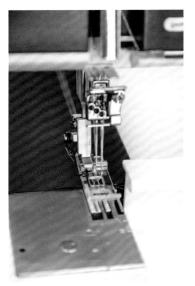

Stitch over previous stitches.
Photo by Katrina Walker

Needles placed just behind previous stitches
Photo by Katrina Walker

To remove the coverstitched fabric from the serger, raise the presser foot and gently but firmly pull the fabric toward the left and back of the machine (at a 45° angle) until the fabric is away from the presser foot.

Trim the excess threads close to the fabric.

TIP // Coverstitch like a Pro
See Chapter 7: Safety Stitch and Coverstitching (page 100) for detailed instructions for beginning and ending coverstitch seams.

Pull fabric out of machine.
Photo by Katrina Walker

CHANGING THREADS WITH THE PULL-THROUGH METHOD

While threading a serger may take some practice, changing the thread on a serger is very easy to do. Start by cutting the serger threads just above the cones.

Next, place the new thread cones in place and tie the new threads on to the tails of the previous threads with a simple overhand or weaver's knot.

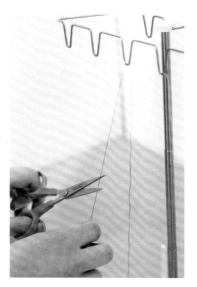

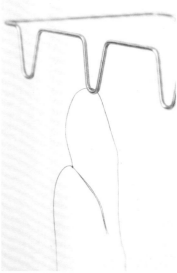

Leave at least a 1″ (2.5cm) tail when tying the knots to ensure that the knot stays secure while traveling through the serger.

Open tension discs, and gently pull the tied threads through the serger loopers. Then pull the needle threads through until they reach the needle(s). Do not try to pull a thread knot through the needle; cut the knot off just before the needle and thread the needle manually.

Threading Decorative Threads

Decorative specialty threads are fabulous for use in serger loopers to create beautiful hems and embellishment. But they can be difficult to thread. The solution? First, thread the serger loopers with regular serger thread. Then tie the decorative thread onto the already threaded looper threads, and gently pull through to rethread the serger. If this is not an option, apply a drop of thread sealant to the end of the bulky decorative thread. Allow it to dry, and then cut the tip of the thread to a sharp threadable point.

TROUBLESHOOTING SERGER STITCHES

Every thread, fabric, and stitch combination is unique. As a result, even with automatic tension sometimes things go a bit awry. Here is a basic tension adjustment chart to help you diagnose and fix common problems.

Serger Tension Adjustment Chart

	Problem	Adjustment
2-thread overlock stitches	Lower looper thread (yellow) lying on the underside of the seam	Increase the lower looper thread tension (yellow) or decrease the needle thread tension (blue or green).
	Needle thread tension (blue or green) pulling toward edge of seam	Increase the needle thread tension (blue or green) or decrease the lower looper thread tension (yellow).
2- or 3-thread wrapped stitches	Needle thread tension (blue or green) pulling toward the edge of the seam	Decrease the lower looper tension (yellow) or increase the needle thread tension (blue or green).
	Loops hanging off the edge or similar indication of loose looper thread (yellow)	Increase the lower looper tension (yellow). If loops are hanging off the edge, also try moving the cutting blade away from the needle.
3-thread flatlock stitches	Lower looper thread (yellow) showing too much in needle or looper stitching	Increase the lower looper thread tension (yellow) or decrease the needle thread tension (blue or green).
	Upper looper thread (red) showing too much in needle or looper stitching	Increase the upper looper thread tension (red) or decrease the needle thread tension (blue or green).
	Needle thread (blue or green) showing too much in looper stitching	Increase the needle thread tension (blue or green) or decrease the upper looper thread tension (red).
3-thread overlock stitches	Upper looper thread (red) showing on underside of seam	Increase the upper looper thread tension (red) or decrease the lower looper thread tension (yellow).
	Lower looper thread (yellow) showing on the upper side of the seam	Increase the lower looper thread tension (yellow) or decrease the upper looper thread tension (red).
	Needle thread too loose	Increase the needle thread tension (blue or green).

	Problem	Adjustment
4-thread overlock stitches	Upper looper thread showing on underside of seam	Increase the upper looper thread tension (red) or decrease the lower looper thread tension (yellow).
	Lower looper showing on upper side of seam	Increase the lower looper thread tension (yellow) or decrease the upper looper thread tension (red).
	Left needle thread (blue) too loose	Increase the left needle thread tension (blue).
	Right needle thread (green) too loose	Increase the right needle tension (green).
5-thread safety stitches	Chain stitching appears loose	Increase the chain-stitch needle thread tension (blue) or decrease the chain-stitch looper thread tension (purple).
	Upper looper thread showing on underside of seam	Increase the upper looper thread tension (red), or decrease the lower looper thread tension (yellow).
	Lower looper showing on upper side of seam	Increase the lower looper thread tension (yellow) or decrease the upper looper thread tension (red).
	Left needle thread (blue) too loose	Increase the left needle thread tension (blue).
	Right needle thread (green) too loose	Increase the right needle tension (green).
Chain stitch	Chain stitching appears loose	Increase the chain-stitch needle thread tension (blue) or decrease the chain-stitch looper thread tension (purple).
Coverstitches	Coverstitch looper thread (purple) appearing on top of fabric (too loose)	Increase the coverstitch looper thread tension (purple).
	Left coverstitch needle thread tension (blue) appearing loose (showing on back of fabric)	Increase the left coverstitch needle tension (blue) or decrease the coverstitch looper thread tension (purple).
	Middle coverstitch needle thread tension (green) appearing loose (showing on back of fabric)	Increase the middle coverstitch needle thread tension (green) or decrease the coverstitch looper thread tension (purple).
	Right coverstitch needle thread tension (red) appearing loose (showing on back of fabric)	Increase the right coverstitch needle thread tension (red) or decrease the coverstitch looper thread tension (purple).
	Top surface of fabric bulging between stitching, and underside stitching looking tight	Decrease the coverstitch looper thread tension (purple).

Stitches

Even the most basic serger can create many stitches. Successful serging comes from understanding which stitches are most effective for a particular fabric or technique. Choosing the most compatible serger stitch depends on several factors such as fabric thickness, desired seam strength, and how much you want the seam to be able to stretch.

The performance characteristics of serger stitches are as diverse as the number of threads, needles, and other elements used to create them. Whether a seam is bulky or lightweight, can stretch or not, or even perform a specialty function like forming a rolled hem or flat seam, depends on how the various machine stitch elements are created. In addition, the tension used for the various loopers and needles also plays a role in stitch formation.

SERGER STITCH PERFORMANCE CHARACTERISTICS

For each serger stitch, the individual components that work together to create the stitch will vary in a unique way. A reference chart is the easiest way to keep track of the way each stitch is set up for stitching, as well as its performance characteristics. A stitch reference chart identifies the components of the machine used for creating the stitch.

Serger Stitch Name:	(1)			4 Thread Overlock				
Needles	Stitch Finger	2 Thread Converter	Cutting Blade	Threading Path / Tension Settings				
Ⓐ Ⓑ Ⓒ Ⓓ Ⓔ	N / R	⟍⟍	Y / N	A	B	U	L	C
(2) A, B	(3) N	(4) No	(5) Yes	(6) *	*	*	*	

Sample Stitch Chart

This sample stitch chart shows the stitch name, the various possible components used, tension settings, and other reference information.

1. Stitch name The common name for the serger stitch.

2. Needle(s) used Overlock needles are labeled *A* (left) and *B* (right); coverstitch needles are labeled *C* (left), *D* (middle), and *E* (right).

3. Stitch finger or stitch plate used *R* for rolled hem setting (stitch finger disengaged or rolled hem stitch plate) or *N* for normal setting (stitch finger engaged or normal stitch plate used).

4. 2-thread converter engaged Yes or no?

5. Cutting blade engaged Yes or no?

6. Thread path used Indicates which threading path is used for needles (positions A and B) and loopers (*U* for upper looper, *L* for lower looper, and *C* for chain-stitch looper). For certain stitches such as the triple coverstitch, a looper tension disk may be used as part of a needle thread path.

Note // Adjusting Stitch Tension
Some sergers automatically set stitch tension for the stitch selected, but these can usually be adjusted for special effects or fabric variations. Manual serger tension settings vary by serger. Check your serger manual for the specific tension settings for your serger.

Tip // Create a Serger Reference Notebook
Print your own personalized serger reference sheets using the chart (page 69) to create a stitch reference of your particular serger's settings. Add stitched samples of each stitch on different fabrics for extra benefit.

2-Thread Stitches

2-thread stitches use special components to create them. The chain stitch requires a chain-stitch looper, found only on 5-thread–capable sergers. Other 2-thread stitches use a converter that hooks into the upper looper, allowing it to be bypassed (only the lower looper is threaded). 2-thread stitches are generally used to avoid thread bulk, such as for lightweight fabrics. They are less strong than 3- or 4-thread stitches.

Suitable for basting and other seams that are intended to be temporary or otherwise reinforced, the chain stitch is strong but it can be unraveled. With decorative thread in the looper and the fabric placed upside down while stitching, the chain stitch can also be used for decorative topstitching.

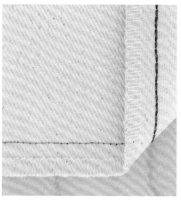

Chain stitch

Suitable for overcasting (seam finishing) a single layer of light- to medium-weight fabric, this stitch can be used for seaming but is not as strong as a 3- or 4-thread stitch.

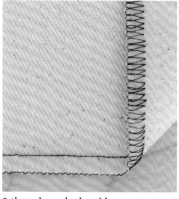

2-thread overlock, wide

This stitch is the same as the 2-thread overlock, except narrower. It is suitable for overcasting a single layer of light- to medium-weight fabric or creating a delicate, narrow seam.

2-thread overlock, narrow

This stitch is suitable as a hem for lightweight fabric.

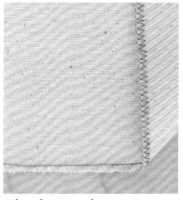

2-thread narrow edge

Suitable for seaming lightweight, medium-weight, or stretchy fabrics together with a flat, nonabrasive seam, the 2-thread wide flatlock can also be used to mimic a blanket-stitched hem.

Tip // Flatlocking Is Fabulous! **Learn more about how to use the 2- and 3-thread flatlock stitches in Chapter 5 (page 88).**

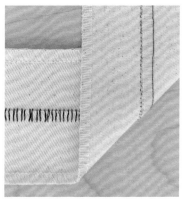

2-thread flatlock, wide

This stitch is the same as the 2-thread flatlock but with a narrower appearance.
It is suitable for seaming lightweight, medium-weight, or stretchy fabrics together with a flat, nonabrasive seam.

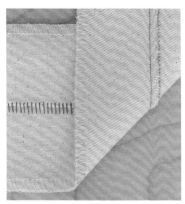

2-thread flatlock, narrow

Suitable as a lightweight but decorative flat hem, this stitch is especially attractive with decorative thread in the looper.

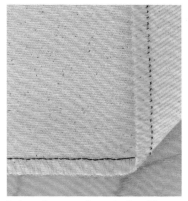

2-thread wrapped overlock, wide

A narrower version of the 2-thread wrapped overlock, this stitch is suitable for a lightweight flat hem.

Tip // Nearly Invisible Hems
The 2-thread wrapped overlock stitch can be used with polyester monofilament thread in the looper for a nearly invisible hem.

2-thread wrapped overlock, narrow

This stitch is suitable for creating a very narrow rolled-edge hem, especially on lightweight fabrics. It may require the stitch length to be shortened or the cutting width to be widened to work well with loosely woven fabrics.

Tip // Finishing Touches
Learn more about creating beautiful serged hems in Chapter 6 (page 94).

2-thread rolled hem

3-Thread Stitches

Most 3-thread stitches use only 1 needle and both upper and lower loopers. They offer greater seam stretch than a 4-thread stitch. The seams they create are less stable or strong than a 4-thread stitch but still provide reasonable seam strength along with stretch compatibility.

This stitch is suitable for seaming light- to medium-weight wovens and knits—especially stretchy knits—and also for overcasting (seam finishing) fabrics.

Tip // Beautiful Braids
The 3-thread overlock stitch can be used to create decorative braid by threading heavy threads through the loopers. Chain off the amount of trim needed.

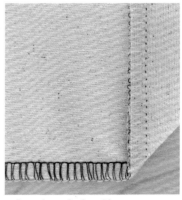

3-thread overlock, wide

This is narrower version of the 3-thread overlock, suitable for seaming light- to medium-weight wovens and knits. The narrower seam is less bulky.

Tip // Fancy Tucks
Create decorative tucks in fabric using the narrow 3-thread overlock. Disengage the cutting blade and stitch along a fabric fold.

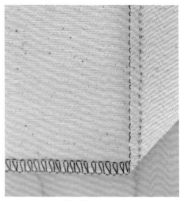

3-thread overlock, narrow

This stitch is suitable for edging (hemming) light- to medium-weight fabrics.
It is not recommended for heavyweight wovens or knits.

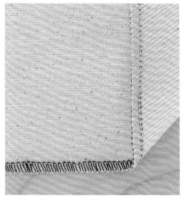

3-thread narrow edge

The 3-thread flatlock is suitable for seaming lightweight, medium-weight, or stretchy fabrics together with a flat, nonabrasive seam—especially for shapewear and sportswear. It is stronger than the 2-thread version.

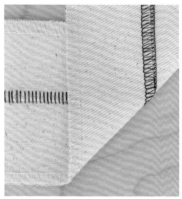

3-thread flatlock, wide

A narrower version of the 3-thread flatlock, this stitch is suitable for seaming lightweight, medium-weight, or stretchy fabrics together with a flat, nonabrasive seam.

Tip // Oh, Baby!
The narrow 3-thread flatlock is ideal for infant wear because of the soft, flat seam structure.

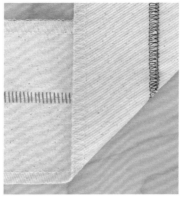

3-thread flatlock, narrow

This stitch is suitable for overcasting (seam finishing) or flat hemming light- to medium-weight fabrics.

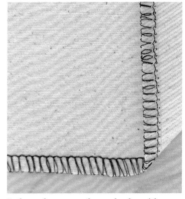

3-thread wrapped overlock, wide

A narrow version of the 3-thread wrapped overlock, this stitch is suitable for overcasting (seam finishing) or flat hemming light- to medium-weight fabrics.

3-thread wrapped overlock, narrow

This stitch is suitable for seaming high-stretch sportswear knits and similar fabrics. Twin needles give extra seam strength, but the single looper (you must use a 2-thread converter) allows greater mobility.

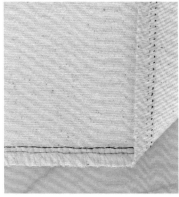

3-thread stretch overlock

Suitable for hemming lightweight fabrics, this stitch creates a slightly heavier rolled hem with more coverage than the 2-thread rolled hem.

3-thread rolled hem

4-Thread Stitches

The 4-thread overlock is the standard 4-thread stitch created by most, if not all, sergers. It creates a sturdy, thread-wrapped seam that also allows some stretch. Some sergers can also create 4-thread variations of a safety stitch seam, but they are only offered on 5-thread capable sergers.

The 4-thread overlock is suitable for seams on all fabrics, especially knits. It creates a very strong seam that also allows stretch, but it creates more bulk due to the 4 threads.

4-thread overlock

A combination of chain-stitched seam with overlocked edge, this stitch creates a reinforced, fray-resistant seam suitable for all fabrics. It requires a serger with both a 2-thread converter and chain-stitch looper.

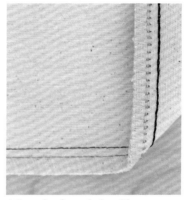

4-thread safety stitch, wide

A narrow version of the 4-thread safety stitch, this stitch is suitable for creating a strong, fray-resistant seam on all fabrics.

Tip // Right Side Up
Coverstitched hems look different on each side of the fabric.

4-thread safety stitch, narrow

5-Thread Stitches

5-thread stitches create the safety stitch seams and coverlock-style hems seen in commercial clothing, especially casual and sportswear. These specialty stitches are only available in 5-thread–capable sergers. Note: Coverlock stitches and 4-thread safety stitches are only offered on 5-thread capable sergers.

This stitch is suitable for creating a strong, reinforced, and overlocked seam on all fabrics. It is the strongest but also most bulky serger seam, commonly seen in commercial garments, especially jeans.

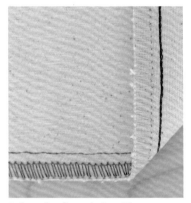

5-thread safety stitch, wide

A narrower version of the 5-thread safety stitch, this stitch is suitable for all fabrics, especially those requiring an especially strong seam.

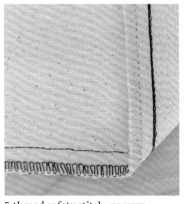

5-thread safety stitch, narrow

A narrower version of the coverstitch, this stitch is suitable for hemming a wide variety of fabrics for many applications. The narrower spacing of the 2 rows of straight stitching is more attractive for smaller or more delicate items.

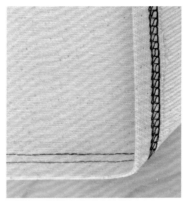

Coverstitch, narrow

The coverstitch is suitable for hemming casual wear, sportswear, and home decor. The top (right side) of the hem shows 2 rows of straight stitches.

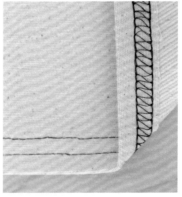

Coverstitch, wide

This stitch is suitable for creating a bold, decorative hem on all fabrics.

Tip // Coverstitching Is Cool
Special tips and techniques for using the coverstitch can be found in Chapter 7 (page 100).

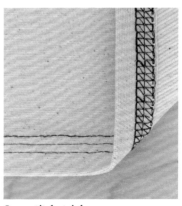

Coverstitch, triple

As You Serge, So Shall You Rip

Serged seams look difficult to rip, but thankfully they are simple to unsew. The trick is to only pick the needle stitches. To do this, cut a needle stitch every few stitches.

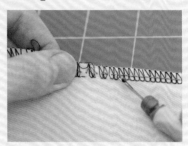

Ripping serger needle stitches

Next, carefully pick and pull out the needle stitches.

Pulling serger needle stitches

Once the needle stitches have been removed, it is easy to gently pull off the looper stitches.

Pulling off looper stitches

SELECTING SERGER STITCHES FOR KNIT AND STRETCH FABRICS

Choosing the most compatible serger stitch for knit fabrics requires taking the fabric performance characteristics into consideration. How thick or heavy is the fabric? Is it stretchy? If so, how stretchy is it? Use the chart below to help choose the most compatible stitches for your fabric.

Fabric Weight	Stretch	Common Fabrics	Suggested Serger Stitches	
			Seams	Hems
Light	Slight to moderate	Lace, stretch charmeuse, tricot	2-thread overlock, narrow or wide 2-thread wrapped overlock, narrow 2-thread flatlock, narrow or wide 3-thread overlock, narrow or wide 3-thread wrapped overlock, narrow or wide 3-thread flatlock, narrow or wide	2-thread flat hem 2-thread narrow edge 2-thread rolled hem 3-thread rolled hem Coverstitch, narrow, wide, or triple
Light	Very stretchy	Stretch lace, tissue jersey, jersey	2-thread overlock, narrow or wide 2-thread wrapped overlock, narrow 2-thread flatlock, narrow or wide 3-thread overlock, narrow or wide 3-thread wrapped overlock, narrow or wide 3-thread flatlock, narrow or wide 3-thread stretch overlock	2-thread flat hem 2-thread narrow edge 2-thread rolled hem 3-thread rolled hem Coverstitch, narrow, wide, or triple
Medium	Slight to moderate	Double-knit, ponte, light-weight fleece, velour	3-thread overlock, narrow or wide 3-thread flatlock, narrow or wide 3-thread stretch overlock 4-thread overlock	2-thread flat hem 2-thread overlock, narrow or wide Coverstitch, narrow, wide, or triple
Medium	Very stretchy	Slinky knit, rib, swimwear, stretch velvet	3-thread overlock, narrow or wide 3-thread flatlock, narrow or wide 3-thread stretch overlock 4-thread overlock	2-thread flat hem 2-thread overlock, narrow or wide Coverstitch, narrow, wide, or triple
Heavy	Slight to moderate	Boiled wool, fleece	3-thread overlock, wide 3-thread stretch overlock 4-thread overlock	Coverstitch, wide or triple
Heavy	Very stretchy	Performance fleece, heavy rib, sweater knit	3-thread overlock, wide 3-thread stretch overlock 4-thread overlock	Coverstitch, wide or triple

SELECTING SERGER STITCHES FOR WOVEN FABRICS

Selecting the most compatible serger stitch for a particular woven fabric is a bit easier than for knits, but the fabric weight and weave structure still need to be considered. Many woven fabrics now also have some stretch ability, but not so much that it should affect the choice of serger stitch the way that a knit fabric's stretch might.

Fabric Weight	Weave Density	Common Fabrics	Suggested Serger Stitches	
			Seams	Hems
Light	Loose	Chiffon, georgette, gauze, handwoven sheers	2-thread chain stitch (basting) 2-thread overlock, narrow or wide 2-thread wrapped overlock, narrow 2-thread flatlock, narrow or wide 3-thread overlock, narrow or wide 3-thread wrapped overlock, narrow or wide 3-thread flatlock, narrow or wide	2-thread flat hem 2-thread narrow edge 2-thread rolled hem 3-thread rolled hem Coverstitch, narrow or wide
Light	Moderate to dense	Handkerchief linen, batiste, windbreaker, silk habotai	2-thread chain stitch (basting) 2-thread overlock, narrow or wide 2-thread wrapped overlock, narrow 2-thread flatlock, narrow or wide 3-thread overlock, narrow or wide 3-thread wrapped overlock, narrow or wide 3-thread flatlock, narrow or wide	2-thread flat hem 2-thread narrow edge 2-thread rolled hem 3-thread rolled hem Coverstitch, narrow, wide, or triple
Medium	Loose	Madras cotton, handwoven linen, silk/rayon velvet	2-thread chain stitch (basting) 2-thread overlock, wide 2-thread flatlock, narrow or wide 3-thread overlock, narrow or wide 3-thread wrapped overlock, narrow or wide 3-thread flatlock, narrow or wide 4-thread overlock 4-thread safety stitch, wide 5-thread safety stitch, wide	2-thread flat hem 3-thread rolled hem 3-thread narrow edge Coverstitch, narrow, wide, or triple

Fabric Weight	Weave Density	Common Fabrics	Suggested Serger Stitches	
			Seams	Hems
Medium	Moderate to dense	Chino, light-weight denim, crepe, light-weight corduroy, flannel, shantung, taffeta, cavalry twill	2-thread chain stitch (basting) 2-thread overlock, narrow or wide 2-thread wrapped overlock, narrow 2-thread flatlock, narrow or wide 3-thread overlock, narrow or wide 3-thread wrapped overlock, narrow or wide 3-thread flatlock, narrow or wide 4-thread overlock 4-thread safety stitch, narrow or wide 5-thread safety stitch, narrow or wide	2-thread flat hem 3-thread rolled hem 3-thread narrow edge Coverstitch, narrow, wide, or triple
Heavy	Loose	Handwoven wool, bouclé	2-thread chain stitch (basting) 3-thread overlock, wide 3-thread flatlock, wide 4-thread overlock 4-thread safety stitch, narrow or wide 5-thread safety stitch, narrow or wide	Coverstitch, narrow, wide, or triple
Heavy	Moderate to dense	Denim, canvas, corduroy, melton	2-thread chain stitch (basting) 3-thread overlock, wide 4-thread overlock 4-thread safety stitch, narrow or wide 5-thread safety stitch, narrow or wide	Coverstitch, narrow, wide, or triple

BUILD A SERGER REFERENCE NOTEBOOK

Use this handy chart to build a reference notebook of your serger stitches and their settings. Place a stitched sample on the page and make notes of any special changes made.

Serger Stitch Reference Chart

Serger Stitch Name:								
Needles	Stitch Finger	2 Thread Converter	Cutting Blade	Threading Path / Tension Settings				
Ⓐ Ⓑ Ⓒ Ⓓ Ⓔ	N / R	🔧	Y / N	A	B	U	L	C

Stitch Sample:		Differential Feed:		Cutting Width:	

Stitch Sample:

Notes:

Serger Skill Building

CHAPTER 4

Serging with Confidence

Now that you have your serger threaded and know which serger stitches to use, it's time to learn how to serge with accuracy and confidence. A little bit of practice using some basic techniques will have you serging along a raw edge or creating a seam effortlessly. Built-in tools such as differential feed make it simple to serge stretchy or unstable fabrics attractively. Even serging curves and corners is easy once you know the techniques.

PREPARING TO SERGE

Creating Accurate Seam Allowances

MARKING THE SEAM ALLOWANCE

The first step toward successful serging is marking an accurate seam allowance. Unlike a traditional sewing machine, the serger blade cuts off any excess seam allowance for most stitches. In addition, the varying finished seam widths created by using different needle positions can easily result in inaccurate sewing.

The variability of serger seam width makes it necessary to confirm your seam allowance for the specific stitch you intend to use, prior to constructing your project. To do this, start by marking the project's seam allowance (for garments, usually ⅝″/1.6cm, and for quilts generally ¼″/6mm) on a scrap of your project fabric. To test a seam, be sure to use 2 layers of fabric together for greatest accuracy.

What Are Serger Stitch Widths?

Serger stitch widths vary slightly depending on the cutting blade depth. Here are the width ranges for serged seams based on the needle used:

Left needle (wide serger seam): 5–7mm (approximately ¼″)

Right needle (narrow serger seam): 3–5mm (approximately ³⁄₁₆″)

Chain-stitch needle (5- or 4-thread safety stitch): 8–10mm (approximately ⅜″)

Left to right: Chain-stitch, left, and right needle-stitch width markings shown on presser foot

Place the fabric with the marked seam allowance against the serger presser foot, with the marked seam allowance aligned with the farthest left needle. If the fabric is heavy, you may need to lift the presser foot and place the fabric slightly under it. Serge a few stitches so that the fabric is being cut by the cutting blade, keeping the marked seam allowance aligned with the needle.

Marked seam allowance set against presser foot

Check your serger foot and the serger cutting guard. Are there marks present that align with the edge of the fabric, and with the needle position? Most sergers have the needle positions marked on the foot. There may also be alignment marks on the cutting blade guard.

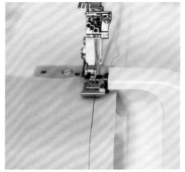

Serging with marked seam allowance aligned accurately

Tip // Make A Seam Allowance Stitching Guide
No seam allowance guide? Create your own seam guide with a narrow piece of removable colored tape (such as painter's tape or designers' ¼"/6mm tape).

With the test fabric still in place, use a piece of removable colored tape or other removable method to mark the alignment of the edge of the fabric. This will give you a visual reference to keep your seam allowance accurate when stitching.

Blue tape placed in alignment with fabric edge

If there are needle alignment marks on your serger presser foot, make a note of which mark aligns with the needle(s) you are using as well. The needle to the furthest left determines the depth of your seam allowance and is where your marked seam allowance should align. Many serger users will find that using a guide to the right of

Alignment marks on presser foot

the cutting blades (or on the bed of the machine when using a coverstitch) is the best visual reference for accuracy. But there may be times when the needle alignment mark is used instead of or in addition to a cutting area seam guide.

BASTING SERGER SEAMS

Many sewing enthusiasts are accustomed to using pins along the stitching line to secure their seams before sewing. Serger cutting blades and presser foot structure make it impossible to use pins in the same way. Thankfully, pins can still be used, but they must either be removed before reaching the cutting blades or placed outside the serging area.

Tip // Pinning for Serging
Yes, you can still use pins! Simply place your pins parallel to the raw edge, to the left of the serger presser foot away from the serging area.

There are many alternatives to using pins when securing your seams and hems for serging.

Wonder Clips (by Clover) are handy to use for serging seams, as they hold edges securely yet are easy to see and remove before reaching the cutting area.

Wonder Clips

Temporary adhesives, such as a washable glue stick, are another handy way to baste serger seam allowances. Wash-away basting tape is also an option, although it should be kept out of the immediate stitching and cutting area, as it can gum up the needles and cutting blades.

Glue stick

Tip // No Glue Zone
Do not use adhesives when serging flatlock seams—they will prevent the seam from being opened flat.

Surprisingly, one of the most effective methods for holding a seam together prior to serging is thread basting using a traditional sewing machine. This is especially true if you need to check the fit of a garment before serging the seam or are serging something challenging like a set-in

Sewing machine basted seam

sleeve. Once a seam is serged, the garment can only be adjusted smaller. If your fabric is slippery or stretchy, machine basting it first using a walking foot or dual feed can make serging much more successful. You can also stitch baste the seam by hand.

Using Differential Feed

Differential feed refers to the adjustable speed of the dual feed dogs under the serger presser foot. Sergers are unique in their ability to change the speed of the front feed dog so that it moves fabric either faster or slower than the rear feed dog.

Differential feed adjustment dial

When the differential feed setting is set above 0 (faster), it can be used to gather fabrics, or to keep knits from being stretched as they're serged.

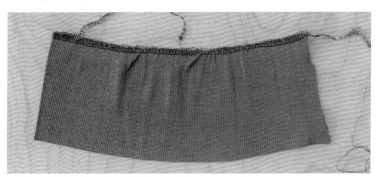

Differential feed causing fabric to gather

Tip // Helping Hands
When gathering with differential feed, gently push the fabric into the serger presser foot. You can also use a finger at the back of the presser foot to slow the fabric from exiting. This helps the serger gather the fabric efficiently.

Setting the differential feed below 0 (slower) helps to keep the fabric taut while serging, which can reduce puckering in tightly woven fabrics, or create decorative effects like "lettuce" edging.

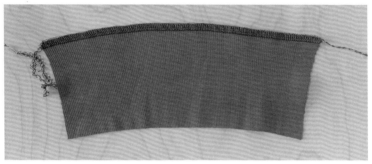
Differential feed causing fabric to stretch

Tip // Differential Feed Fun
Learn how to use differential feed to create fancy lettuce edged hems and seams in Chapter 8 (page 111).

SERGING A BASIC SEAM OR FINISH

When learning to serge, thread your serger with a basic 4-thread overlock stitch to practice. Once your serger is threaded and the stitch has been successfully tested, you are ready to serge!

There should be a thread chain 4″ (10.2cm) or longer to start. Be sure the thread chain is to the back of the serger foot so that it will not become tangled when the serger starts to stitch. Place the fabric against the front of the serger presser foot, either with the raw edge  aligned with the cutting blade (edge stitching) or with the seam guide (seaming with a seam allowance).

Tip // Need a Lift?
If the fabric is thick, you may need to lift the presser foot to place your fabric before starting a seam.

Gently press on the foot control to start serging. Allow the serger to feed the fabric under the presser foot, only guiding if necessary.

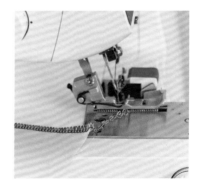

Serge to the end of the fabric and chain off by gently pulling the fabric to the back of the serger while stitching off the fabric. Create a thread chain at least 5″ (12.7cm) long.

Cut the chain about 2″ (5.1cm) from the end of the fabric. Secure the thread chains on the fabric at the beginning and end of the seam using a thread sealant, knotting the chains, or threading the chains back through the stitching.

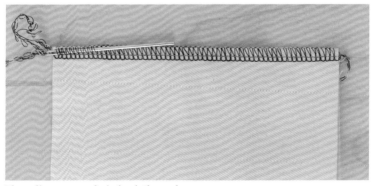

Threading serger chain back through

Serging Curves

Both concave and convex curves can be easily serged, but they each require a different handling technique to ensure stitch accuracy.

Serging Curves With Seam Allowances

Starting a serged seam on a curve or a circle can be challenging due to the need to accommodate the cutting blade. Here are two ways to address this challenge. The first method is to determine the cutting line of the seam allowance and trim a notch along the cutting line long enough to be able to start the seam on the needles without having excess fabric caught beside the cutting blade (usually about 1½"/3.8cm).

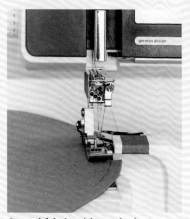

Curved fabric with notch along cutting line

The second method is to mark the cutting line for the seam allowance, and precut the fabric along that line, eliminating the need for the cutting blade to trim the allowance. This takes more time but may be a more comfortable choice when first learning to use a serger.

Precutting curved fabric along cutting line

Tip // Slow It Down!
Sergers don't have to be fast. Use the speed control to slow the serger down to a comfortable pace.

Convex, or outward, curves are perhaps the easiest curves to serge. Position your hand to the left of the serger so that it can help to pivot the fabric around the curve as you serge. Practice overcasting or hemming around the edge of curves first.

Serging convex curve

As you are serging, the curve of the fabric should be just skimming along the edge of the cutting blade without being cut. Once you are comfortable with being able to serge along the edge of an outside curve, seaming on a curve will be easier.

Serging curve with fabric skimming blade

Why Use The Cutting Blade?

The cutting blade can be lowered or disengaged while serging. So why use it when serging fabric edges? The cutting blade ensures that the raw edge is the correct distance from the loopers for successful stitch formation. Learn to use it as a guide rather than disengage it and risk poor stitch quality.

CONCAVE CURVES

Serging a concave, or inward, curve successfully requires maneuvering the fabric to avoid the curve being cut by the blade. Practice overcasting or hemming along the edge of the curve first. When practicing this for the first time, you can disengage the cutting blade.

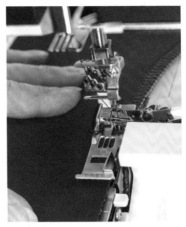

Serging concave curve

As you serge, you will gently straighten the concave curve by rotating the portion in front of the serger to the left. It is important to avoid stretching the fabric as you move it. Straighten the fabric just enough to avoid the cutting blades while overcasting or hemming. When seaming, focus on keeping the straightened fabric edge aligned with the seam allowance alignment marks.

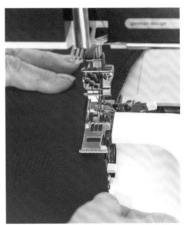

Concave curve being straightened while serging

Serging in Circles

Serging a continuous circle is very similar to serging a convex (outward) curve. A circle is serged by keeping the edge of the circle skimming along the edge of the cutting blade without being cut. The cutting blade can be disengaged if necessary. Seaming along a circular edge may require precutting a notch along the cutting line in order to start the seam or trimming away the extra seam allowance on the cutting line prior to serging.

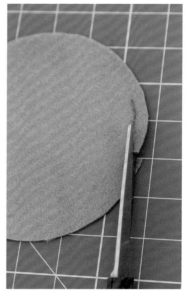

Precutting notch on circle for starting seam

Serging Corners

As with curves, there are 2 types of corners: outside corners and inside corners. Both can be successfully serged but require very different techniques.

SERGING AN OUTSIDE CORNER

Serging an outside corner is simple, requiring only a choice of whether to chain off at the corner, or serge it as a continuous operation.

Chaining-Off Method

The chaining off method is the easiest way to serge an outside corner. To do this, simply serge straight past the corner and chain off.

Serging chain extending past edge

Insert the second side of the corner into the serger, as you normally would start a seam or hem. Continue to serge.

Starting second side of corner

The finished corner will have a thread chain extending from it. Secure the thread chain using a sealant or by threading the chain back through the overlock stitches.

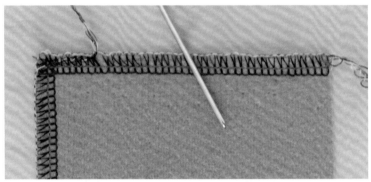

Securing thread chain by threading through overlock stitches

Continuous Outer-Corner Serging

Serging an outside corner as a continuous stitch is not difficult but does take more practice than the chaining off method. To do this, serge to the corner, stopping when the serger needles are just off the fabric, about 1–2 stitches.

Serger needles stopped just past corner

Tip // The Handwheel Is Handy
Use the handwheel when beginning a chain after threading or turning a corner. It is the best way to maintain slow control over stitch formation.

With the presser foot lifted, and needles up, gently pull the chain off the stitch needles.

Rotate the fabric so that the second side of the corner is now under the needles, and the edge of the fabric is flush against the cutting blade.

Rotate second side of corner into place.

If you have a seam allowance that needs to be trimmed from the second side of the corner, snip on the cutting line approximately 1″ (2.5cm) before rotating the fabric into place so that the excess fabric is not caught in the blade.

Once the fabric is in place, continue serging away from the corner.

Continue serging away from corner.

SERGING AN INSIDE CORNER

Serging an inner corner simply requires a little advanced preparation to create a perfectly formed corner. Before serging, mark the seam allowance starting 1″ (2.5cm) on either side of the inner corner.

Mark seam allowances.

Clip from the corner toward the marked seam allowance corner, stopping ⅛″ (3mm) away from the marked corner.

Clip marked seam allowance corner.

Start serging toward corner, stopping just before the blade meets the corner. Make sure the needles are down in the fabric to keep it from shifting.

Stop just short of inside corner.

Gently straighten the corner so that it forms a straight line with a small notch at the center of the corner.

Serge through the corner, being careful to keep the fabric straight. Avoid shifting the fabric too far to the left, as this will cause loose loops to form along the edge of the corner.

Continue serging as you normally would. If a small crease or wrinkle has formed at the corner it will smooth out when pressed.

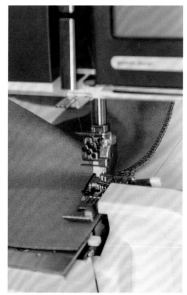

Serge through straightened corner.

SECURING SERGER THREADS

Sergers leave a thread chain at the end of every seam, hem, or overcast that must be secured. This is easily done by using one of 3 different methods:

Method 1 Thread the chain back into the seam using a large eyed needle or bodkin. This is a very tidy method of securing the chain.

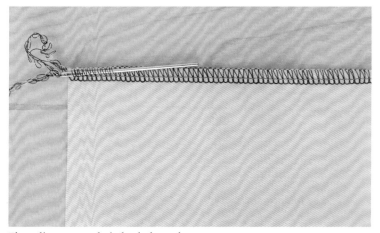

Threading serger chain back through seam

Method 2 Knot the end of the chain next to the edge of the fabric and trim off the excess. This is a quick technique, but the knot can add bulk, so is not suitable for every seam.

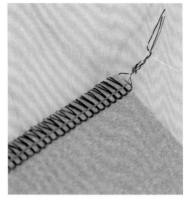

Knot end of thread chain and trim.

Method 3 Use a drop of thread sealant on the chain at the edge of the fabric to prevent fraying. Once the sealant dries, cut off the excess thread chain. This is the least bulky method but the sealant can be messy and adds a bit of stiffness to the end of the seam. Test first on a scrap of fabric and be careful to use only a very small amount.

Use drop of thread sealant.

Serger
Specialty
Stitches

CHAPTER 5

Flatlocking

The flatlock serger stitch is one of the most diverse stitches in the serger repertoire. It creates a uniquely flat seam that is attractive and comfortable to wear. This seam structure makes it suitable for a broad range of applications, from sportswear to infant wear, and even lingerie. In addition, its stitch formation can be used for decorative details such as topstitching, and to create attractive hems.

SETTING UP THE FLATLOCK STITCH

There are 2 types of flatlock stitches: the 2-thread flatlock and 3-thread flatlock. Both use only 1 needle, so the flatlock can be wide or narrow, depending on whether the left or right needle is used. The 2-thread flatlock uses only the lower looper and requires a converter to close the upper looper to form the stitch.

Needles	Stitch Finger	2 Thread Converter	Cutting Blade	Threading Path / Tension Settings				
2 Thread Flatlock (Wide and Narrow)								
				A	B	U	L	C
Ⓐ Ⓑ Ⓒ Ⓓ Ⓔ	N / R	[converter image]	Y / N	A	B	U	L	C
A (wide) B (narrow)	N	Yes	Yes	*W	*N		*	
3 Thread Flatlock (Wide and Narrow)								
Needles	Stitch Finger	2 Thread Converter	Cutting Blade	Threading Path / Tension Settings				
				A	B	U	L	C
Ⓐ Ⓑ Ⓒ Ⓓ Ⓔ	N / R	[converter image]	Y / N	A	B	U	L	C
A (wide) B (narrow)	N	No	Yes	*W	*N	*	*	

Setting chart for 2- and 3-thread flatlock

USING THE FLATLOCK STITCH

Selecting which flatlock to use for your project depends on the fabric used and the seam strength required. If you are flatlocking a delicate fabric, a narrow 2-thread flatlock using lightweight thread is the least conspicuous choice. By contrast, a flatlock seam intended for a swimsuit or sports jersey must be reasonably rugged to withstand stress in multiple directions, so a wide 3-thread flatlock would be an ideal choice.

Flatlock seams also offer decorative opportunities to serger projects. The ladder stitch that is formed on the inside of the seam (the outside or right side of the project if sewn with right sides together) is attractive when sewn with decorative threads, and if a wide flatlock is used, can be used to thread ribbon accents or other trims.

Ribbon insertion

Conversely, the overlock loops that appear on the back side of the seam create a sporty look, especially when used as a topstitching effect. Simply seam with wrong sides together to create this effect.

Overlock loops on right side of fabric

Flatlock Topstitching

Topstitching on a serger? Why not? The flatlock stitch is fun to use as a decorative stitch accent.

1. Disengage the cutting blade.

2. Fold the fabric along the stitching line. Fold right sides together to create a ladder stitch decoration. Fold wrong sides together to show the looper stitches instead.

3. Stitch along the fold.

Stitch along fabric fold.

4. Open up the fabric to show decorative stitching.

Creating a Blind Hem

In addition, the flatlock stitch can be used to create special hems and edge finishes. An attractive blind hem is created by folding up the hem of your project, then folding down the project (toward the right side, creating a Z curve). The cutting blade and loopers are aligned with the top raw edge of the hem, with the needle just passing through the curve where the project folds down at the top of the hem.

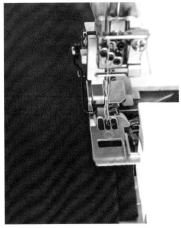

Blind hem folded and correctly aligned with serger foot

Serge along the fold, using the flatlock needle to secure the hem, with the cutting blade trimming any excess fabric from the hem raw edge. Once the hem is complete, pull the flatlock open to flatten the hem, and press.

Tip // Test First!
Always test any serging seam, hem, or technique on scraps of your project fabric before serging.

Creating a Mock Blanket Stitch

A mock blanket stitch edge finish is another fun way to use the wide flatlock stitch. Set up the serger for a wide flatlock and lengthen the stitch to its longest setting. Set the fabric or project in the serger, right side up, with a piece of wash-away stabilizer on top. For non-washable fabrics a heat-away or lightweight tear-away stabilizer may work, but test first.

Serge the fabric and stabilizer together, as if creating a seam. When finished serging, use the stabilizer to pull the needle threads to the outside edge of the fabric, creating a blanket-stitched look.

Stabilizer used to pull stitches to fabric edge

TROUBLESHOOTING THE FLATLOCK STITCH

A correctly stitched flatlock seam lies smooth and flat, just as the name implies. A flatlock stitch is formed by using loose needle thread tension, which allows the seam to be pulled open. Sometimes fabric thickness or variations in thread cause the seam to form a ridge when pulled open, rather than lying flat. There are 2 possible solutions to this problem. First, check the blade cutting depth. Ideally, the flatlock looper threads should be slightly overhanging the edge of the seam. This allows space for the fabric to lie under the loops when the seam is pulled open.

Flatlocking with loops lying loose over the edge

Adjust the blade depth closer to the needles (making a deeper cut) and test the seam again. Second, check the needle thread tension. The needle thread tension needs to be loose enough to accommodate the width of the flatlocked seam. Loosen the needle thread tension and test again. Also check to ensure that any basting stitches have been removed. If these solutions do not fix the problem, your fabric may be too heavy to flatlock correctly.

CHAPTER 6

Rolled Hems

Rolled hems are arguably the loveliest of the serger stitches. The ability to create an attractive thread-wrapped hem quickly and easily is a compelling reason to own a serger. Rolled hems can be used for more than just plain hemming. They also make a decorative seam for delicate fabrics, and create a fun lettuce edging when paired with differential feed.

SETTING UP THE ROLLED HEM

The rolled hem can be created using either 2 or 3 threads. Both versions use the right needle only, but the 2-thread rolled hem requires an upper looper converter. The hem is "rolled" by moving the stitch finger out of the stitch formation area, decreasing the upper looper tension, and increasing the lower looper tension to create a narrow, looper-wrapped stitch. Most sergers use a movable stitch finger that is simply slid back, although some may use a separate rolled hem stitch plate or have you remove the stitch finger completely.

2 Thread Rolled Hem								
Needles	Stitch Finger	2 Thread Converter	Cutting Blade	Threading Path / Tension Settings				
				A	B	U	L	C
[A][B] [C][D][E]	N/R		Y/N	A	B	U	L	C
B A (wide) B (narrow)	R	Yes	Yes		*		*	
3 Thread Rolled Hem								
Needles	Stitch Finger	2 Thread Converter	Cutting Blade	Threading Path / Tension Settings				
				A	B	U	L	C
[A][B] [C][D][E]	N/R		Y/N	A	B	U	L	C
B	R	No	Yes		*	*	*	

Setting chart for 2- and 3-thread rolled hem

USING THE ROLLED HEM

As the name suggests, the rolled hem stitch is generally used for creating a hem on a variety of light to medium weight fabrics. The rolled hem does not work well on heavier fabrics, although a narrow edge finish may be created. The 2-thread rolled hem is a particularly lightweight hem that is lovely when used on scarf fabrics and similar lightweight materials.

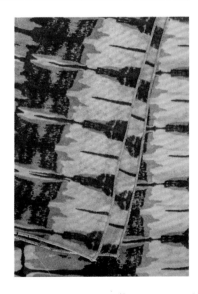

The 3-thread rolled hem provides more weight and extra coverage that looks great for hemming napkins and other fabrics. It is especially attractive when the loopers are threaded with decorative threads.

Rolled hems using rayon thread, texturized nylon, serger yarn, and 12-weight cotton thread

Whenever you create a rolled hem you will want to serge test samples on scrap fabric first. The stitch length, looper tensions, and cutting blade depth may all need to be adjusted for the most attractive results. This is especially true when using decorative threads. Always test before serging your project.

How Much Coverage?

Serger rolled hems wrap the edge of the fabric with thread. How completely the edge is wrapped is a matter of personal preference. The amount of coverage can be adjusted by shortening or lengthening the stitch length. The more thread used for the hem, generally the stiffer the hem will be. This is not an issue for a napkin but could be a concern for a chiffon scarf. To create greater coverage with less bulk, consider using a specialty thread such as texturized ("wooly") nylon or polyester.

Creating a Lettuce-Edge Hem

The lettuce-edge hem is a fun variation of the rolled hem that can be created with stretch fabrics. It uses the stretching capability of the differential feed to intentionally stretch and distort the edge of the fabric while stitching.

Set the serger for a rolled hem as instructed by your manual. Decrease the differential feed to its lowest (slowest) setting. Cut a test fabric strip at least 5″ (12.7cm) long. Chain off a long enough chain to be able to grasp it (approximately 4″/10.2cm) and insert your test fabric.

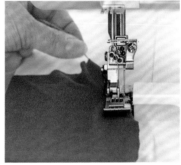

Test fabric inserted into serger

Start to serge the test strip, holding onto the serger chain in back of the serger with your left hand. Once a few stitches have been made into the test strip, continue to serge while gently maintaining a slight tension with your right hand on the test strip in front of the serger.

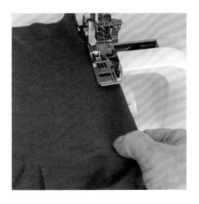

Tip // No Tug of War!
Maintain just enough tension on the fabric to encourage the edge of the fabric to stretch. Pulling too hard will cause skipped stitches or uneven stitch coverage.

Using both the differential feed combined with gentle hand stretching creates the most dramatic lettuce edging. Use your test scraps to practice and determine how much stretch you need for the most attractive results.

Tip // More Thread, Please!
Shorten the stitch length slightly when stitching lettuce-edge hems if the thread coverage looks skimpy.

TROUBLESHOOTING THE ROLLED HEM

While rolled hems are generally easy to serge, they can require some small adjustments to make them look their best. One common issue with rolled hems is inadequate thread coverage, which makes the hem look poorly covered.

To correct this, shorten the stitch length. If a fully covered look is wanted, using a texturized or similar fuzzy thread will also increase the thread coverage.

Another common problem is uneven hems resulting from the fabric not rolling properly.

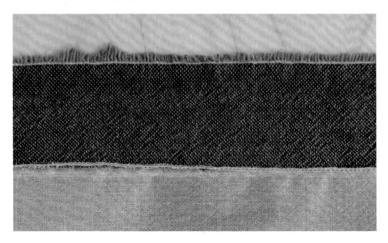

There are two ways to address this problem. First, check the looper tension settings. The upper looper should be loose enough for the lower looper to pull it to the back of the fabric. The tension setting for the lower looper should be tight enough to pull the lower looper to the back of the fabric.

Back side of rolled hem showing looper threads

Tip // No Whiskers!
Threads sticking out of a rolled hem are unattractive. A trick for preventing whiskers in rolled hems is to starch the hemline with spray starch before serging.

Another possible cause for poor fabric rolling can be the cutting blade distance. Increase the width of the fabric edge by adjusting the blade further from the needles. This introduces more fabric into the hem. If the hem is not forming because of too much fabric, decrease the amount of fabric by adjusting the blade closer to the needles.

CHAPTER 7

Safety Stitch and Coverstitching

5-thread–capable sergers create specialty stitches and hems that are unique to them. The 5-thread safety stitch and coverstitch are the 2 stitches most commonly used. While both stitch types use a chain-stitch looper to form their stitches, the 5-thread safety stitch is strictly a construction (seaming) stitch, whereas the coverstitch is used primarily for hemming.

SETTING UP THE 5–THREAD SAFETY STITCH

The 5-thread safety stitch is a combination of an overlock stitch and a chain stitch. The chain stitch forms the actual seam, with the overlock stitches providing extra security in case the chain stitch is broken or unraveled. As a result, the serger is threaded as a combination of a chain stitch, using 1 coverstitch needle and the chain-stitch looper, and a 3-thread overlock, using 1 overlock needle and the upper and lower loopers. This creates a very sturdy, strong seam.

5 Thread Safety Stitch								
Needles	Stitch Finger	2 Thread Converter	Cutting Blade	Threading Path / Tension Settings				
Ⓐ Ⓑ Ⓒ Ⓓ Ⓔ	N / R		Y / N	A	B	U	L	C
D A (wide) B (narrow)	N	No	Yes	*	*	*	*	*

Setting chart for 5-thread safety stitch

USING THE 5–THREAD SAFETY STITCH

The 5-thread safety stitch is serged much like an overlock stitch, with one exception. The 5-thread safety stitch, because it uses a chain stitch, must initially be started with the needles in the fabric. After threading, place a piece of scrap fabric at least 4″ (10.2cm) long under the needles.

Turn the handwheel a few times to gently start while holding the looper and needle threads behind the presser foot. Use the foot pedal to slowly serge a test seam while continuing to hold the threads. The chain stitch may take a few inches to start forming correctly.

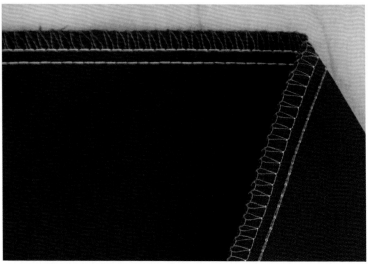

Correctly formed 5-thread safety stitch

Once the chain stitch is forming normally, it can be chained off the edge of a seam the same as a standard overlock stitch.

Use the 5-thread safety stitch whenever you want a strong, stable (non-stretchy) seam, whether for wovens or knits. This is a seam commonly seen in commercially made jeans and other sturdy garments.

TROUBLESHOOTING THE 5-THREAD SAFETY STITCH

The most common problem with the 5-thread safety stitch is the stitch not forming correctly. This generally results from either the serger being threaded incorrectly, or the stitch not being started with the needles in fabric.

Tip // When in Doubt, Rethread
Most serger errors result from sergers being threaded incorrectly, and in the wrong order. If stitches are not forming correctly, unthread the serger and start again. This includes the needles!

Another issue that might be encountered is the overlock loops hanging over the edge of the fabric, or the fabric curling up at the edge.

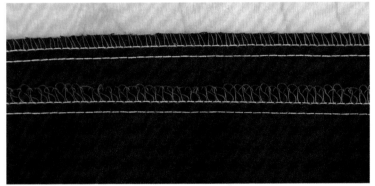

5-thread safety stitch with overlock loops hanging over edge and with fabric curling

In both cases, the problem is corrected by adjusting the cutting blade. If the overlock loops are extending over the edge, widen the fabric edge by adjusting the cutting blade away from the needles. If the fabric is curling, there is too much fabric in the seam. Narrow the seam by adjusting the cutting blade closer to the needles. Always test first! See more troubleshooting tips on page 52.

SETTING UP THE COVERSTITCH

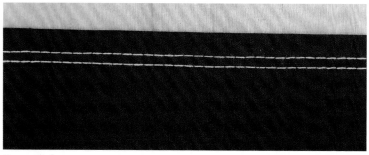

Coverstitch

The coverstitch is used primarily for creating strong and stretchable hems, although it can also be used for decorative topstitching. It uses 2 to 3 needles and a chain-stitch looper to create the hem, with rows of straight stitching on the top side, and a looper chain on the back.

Coverstitch (Wide)								
Needles	Stitch Finger	2 Thread Converter	Cutting Blade	Threading Path / Tension Settings				
Ⓐ Ⓑ Ⓒ Ⓓ Ⓔ	N / R		Y / N	A	B	U	L	C
C, E	N	No	Yes	*	*			*

Setting chart for coverstitch

USING THE COVERSTITCH

A coverstitch is very different from the other serger stitches because it must be started with fabric under the needles. Also, unlike most serger stitches, during coverstitching the cutting blade is disengaged, so the depth of the hem is not automatically determined. The coverstitch is a topstitching technique.

To start a coverstitch after threading, lift the presser foot and place the front of a piece of scrap fabric or stabilizer at least 3″ (7.6cm) long under the needles.

Coverstitching Accurate Hems

Coverstitching does not use a cutting blade, so the depth of the coverstitch hem or stitching line is not as obvious as with other stitches.

Use a seam guide or marking to ensure that your hem coverstitching is accurate and consistent. The coverstitch cover plate usually has hem guide markings, but they may be difficult to read.

Coverstitch cover plate with markings
Photo by Katrina Walker

Some brands offer specialty coverstitching feet or hem guides to make alignment easier. Removable tape can be used to create a temporary guide. Before hemming, measure the hem depth and set any guides or markings accordingly.

Tape hem guide used with coverstitch
Photo by Katrina Walker

CREATING A CONSISTENT HEM FOLD

A hem guide is useless if the hem depth is not folded consistently. Try this technique for temporarily stabilizing hems and making them easy to fold:

1. Determine the hem depth and cut strips of wash-away self-adhesive stabilizer the same width as the hem depth. Cut enough to have a strip for each side of the hem.

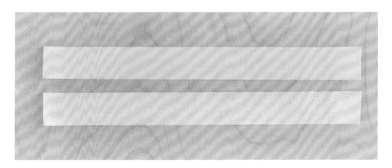

2. Place stabilizer strips on hem in pairs, with one piece aligned with the raw edge of the knit, and the second placed next to it. This allows the hem to fold on the small gap between strips.

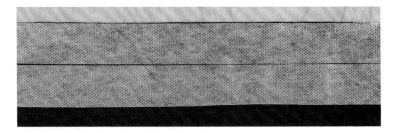

3. Fold the hem up toward the wrong side along the gap between strips and secure.

Tip // Stick That Hem
Temporarily hold hems in place with washable glue stick or light-weight fusible web. Works like a charm!

4. Hem the garment using the coverstitch. When the garment is completed, wash away the stabilizers and glue stick residue.

Tip // Save Scraps—Use Stabilizer!
Use pieces of tear-away stabilizer instead of fabric scraps to start and stop your coverstitching.

Coverstitching in a Line

When coverstitching in a straight line from edge to edge you must start the coverstitch with fabric under the needles. The easiest way to do this is to start on a piece of scrap fabric or tear-away stabilizer. Then simply coverstitch from the stabilizer or scrap onto your fabric.

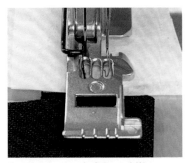

Starting coverstitch in stabilizer
Photo by Katrina Walker

Coverstitches are very easy to unravel from the end of the seam, so they must be secured when finishing. The most secure method is backstitching.

1. Stop just before sewing off the end of the fabric and release the needle thread tension.

---

2. Pull the needle threads so that there is a small amount of slack. Raise the presser foot and pull the fabric off the stitch needles, then forward again so that the needles are placed behind the last few stitches at the end of the hem.

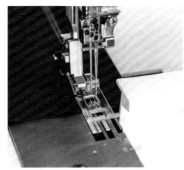

Needles placed behind previous stitches
Photo by Katrina Walker

---

3. Coverstitch again over a few of the previous stitches to lock the coverstitches.

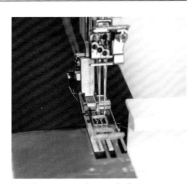

Stitch over previous stitches.
Photo by Katrina Walker

Raise the presser foot and gently but firmly pull the fabric toward the left and back of the machine (at a 45° angle) until the fabric is away from the presser foot.

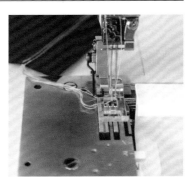

Photo by Katrina Walker

Trim the excess threads close to the fabric.

It is less secure but easiest to end the coverstitch by stitching off onto another piece of stabilizer or fabric. Gently tear the stabilizer or cut the scrap fabric away and secure your threads.

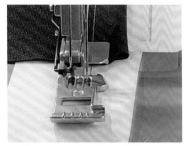

Ending coverstitch in stabilizer
Photo by Katrina Walker

Coverstitching in the Round

When coverstitching a hem in the round, the hem is positioned in place under the needles prior to starting. The coverstitching will overlap itself at the starting/ending point, so choose an inconspicuous place to begin and end your hem, such as at a side or shoulder seam.

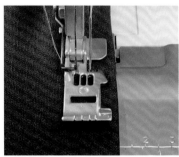

Starting coverstitch hem
Photo by Katrina Walker

Start the hem with the hem positioned under the serger presser foot.

Stitch the hem all the way around. When you reach your starting point, stitch over the beginning stitches so that the stitches overlap. Raise the serger presser foot and loosen the needle threads enough to remove the fabric from underneath the foot.

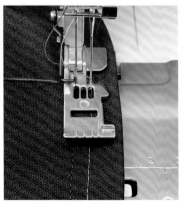

Loosening needle threads
Photo by Katrina Walker

Gently but firmly pull the hem to the side and back, out of the serger. Pull the needle threads to the back of the fabric, secure and trim.

Finished coverstitch hem

TROUBLESHOOTING THE 5–THREAD SAFETY STITCH AND COVERSTITCH

Incorrect threading is the main cause of problems with the 5-thread safety stitch and the coverstitch. Always be careful to thread the loopers first and in the correct order. For the 5-thread safety stitch that normally means the upper looper, then lower looper, then chain-stitch looper.

Tip // The Manual Is Always Right
Although many sergers use the same threading order, always check the manual to ensure the correct order for your particular serger.

The coverstitch only uses the chain-stitch looper. Once the chain-stitch looper is threaded, thread the needles in order from right to left.

Needle thread tension must be correct. If the coverstitch is not lying flat or is puckering, the needle thread tensions may be too tight. If the needle thread is showing prominently on the reverse side, the needle thread tensions may be too loose.

5-thread safety stitches and coverstitches must both be started in fabric or stabilizer. When this step is neglected, the stitch may not form, or only partially form.

The 5-thread safety stitch must always be started with the needles in the fabric after threading, but it can be chained off after successful test stitching.

The coverstitch must be started with the needles in fabric or stabilizer every time, not just after threading. The stitch must end with the needles in fabric or having just finished a stitch (no stitching in the air). Otherwise the stitch may not form.

Serger
Construction
Techniques

CHAPTER 8

Knit Construction Techniques

Sergers can be used to construct any kind of sewing project, whether piecework, fashion, or home decor. The diversity of serger stitches allows the serger to create beautiful seams, seam finishes, and hems on all weights and types of fabric. Successful serging with knits, wovens, and delicates is easy to achieve with just a bit of practice.

Sergers are wonderful for constructing knit garments. First of all, sergers create a strong, stretchable seam. Differential feeding allows stretchy knits to be serged without distorting the fabric. Plus, sergers are fast! It all adds up to make serging knitwear fun, fast, and easy.

CHOOSING A COMPATIBLE STITCH

The first step of successful knit serging is choosing the most compatible stitch for your project.

Knit Stitch Chart

Using a stitch reference chart (page 67) makes it easier to achieve successful results, but there is no substitute for testing the stitches first. Take the time to test your chosen fabric/stitch combination for seam strength and stretchability. It is also an opportunity to see if you like the way the seam looks and whether it will press attractively. The small amount of time spent in preparation will yield much more satisfactory results during construction.

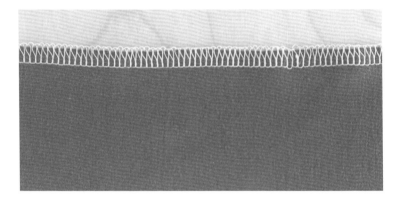

Tip // Test, Test, Test!
Always test your serger settings using scrap fabric from your serger project. Save the test results, noting any adjustments to serger settings in a Serger Reference Chart (page 69), for future reference.

Testing for Stretch and Strength

Serging seams on knit fabrics always requires special testing due to the potential amount of stretch needed during wear. This is especially true of knit fabrics being used for sportswear, where both stretchability and strength must be taken into consideration.

Perform this test as part of your standard fabric and stitch compatibility test before serging. The stitch you use will depend on what is most likely to work well for the project. For example, a 3-thread wide overlock stitch is a good place to start for a project requiring a lot of stretch.

To test for stretch, first cut 2 strips at least 3″ (7.6cm) wide by 6″ (15.2cm) long of scrap fabric from your intended project. If possible, cut the strips lengthwise in the direction of greatest stretch, usually the crosswise direction. Place the strips together, and serge a seam along one long edge. Grasp each short edge of the fabric and pull, to test the amount of stretch.

Pull fabric lengthwise to stretch.

Evaluate the results. Did it stretch adequately? Was the seam strong enough for the use you intend? If not, test a different stitch.

Tip // Taming Tricky Knits

Jersey knits curl along the edges, making seaming and hemming a challenge. Tame them with a bit of spray starch or liquid (wash-away) stabilizer for easier serging. If the fabric is especially unstable, stabilize before cutting. Using a washable glue stick to baste seam allowances together also works beautifully.

3-Thread Or 4-Thread?

Many serging enthusiasts set their sergers for a 4-thread overlock and rarely, if ever, change the threading pattern. This is unfortunate, as there are advantages to using a 3-thread overlock for many applications. It generally has greater stretch, is less bulky, and uses less thread. But sometimes more stability (less stretch) is desirable or greater seam strength might be required. In general, the 4-thread overlock is stronger and more stable than 3-thread stitch options. Use whichever stitch suits your project needs best.

Using Differential Feed

The second set of tests to perform before serging knits involves the differential feed. Knits can be challenging to sew due to the seams being unintentionally stretched out of shape while stitching. The serger's differential feed helps to correct this problem by changing the speed of the front feed dog.

Generally, when serging knits, the differential feed is set at 0 (same speed as back feed dog), or higher, so that the front feed dog is pushing fabric under the serger presser foot faster than the rear feed dog is pulling it out. This keeps the seam from being stretched out of shape.

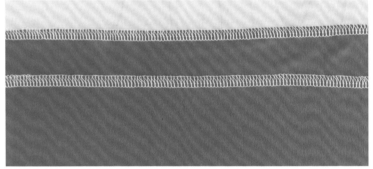

2 test knit pieces with regular (neutral or 0 setting) on the right and increased differential feed (5 setting) on the left

Tip // Distorted by Design
Use the differential feed to stretch a knit rolled hem into a fancy lettuce edging. See Creating a Lettuce-Edge Hem (page 97) for details.

Serge test pieces using various differential feed settings to determine the most compatible setting. Start with the differential feed set at neutral, and if the seam is stretched, increase the feeding speed until the seam lies flat and undistorted.

Always Fit First

Serger seams are easy to sew, but more difficult to alter than sewn seams. It is important to make all of your fit adjustments before serging a garment.

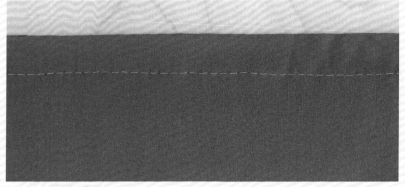

Seam basted for fitting

One way to do this is to baste the seams first using a traditional sewing machine. Use a long straight stitch to baste the garment seams on the intended seam allowance. If your sewing machine has difficulty sewing knit fabric, use a walking foot attachment or dual feed mechanism. Once the seam is basted the garment may be tried on for fit and easily adjusted as necessary. You can leave the basting stitches in place while serging as a stitching guide. Remove the basting stitches after serging if necessary.

SERGING KNITWEAR DETAILS

Knit garments are constructed much the same as woven garments in terms of basic seaming. But knitwear traditionally uses specialty trims for finishing necklines, sleeves, and hemlines. The trims vary depending on what is in fashion. Ribbed collars, cuffs, and waistbands are still found in sportswear, particularly sweatshirts, but knit fashions use a greater variety of trims, including delicate velvet or satin elastic binding or even stretch ribbon. Simple turn-and-stitch hems using a coverstitch have enjoyed a long popularity as well.

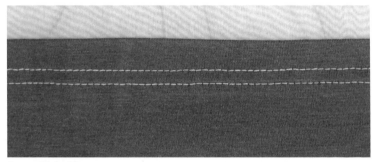

Coverstitched hem

The Quartering System

The basic technique for applying a stretch trim such as ribbing to a knit edge is called quartering. The trim should be evenly distributed around the opening so that it lies smoothly. Marking the trim and garment opening into equal quarters makes it easier to stretch the trim uniformly. Here are the steps to quartering trim:

1. The garment opening is folded in half to find the half measurements of the opening. Sometimes a garment is the same measurement across the front and back, in which case the side seams might be used to mark the 2 halves. But this is not always the case.

Opening marked in halves

2. Fold the garment opening again, this time aligning the half markings, to find the halfway point between each marking. These are the quartering marks.

Opening marked to show quarters

---

3. If applying the trim in the round, serge the joining seam of the trim so that it is circular. If using a flat-construction technique you may leave it in a strip before quartering. To quarter the trim, first fold the trim in half. Mark the halves on the trim.

Trim folded in half and marked

4. Fold the trim on the marks to find the halfway point between the halves. Mark these quartering marks on the trim.

Trim with quartering marks

5. Place the trim around the opening, right sides together and raw edges aligned. Pin the trim to the opening, matching all quartering marks. The trim will need to be stretched around the opening.

Trim pinned in place

6. Attach the trim to the opening, gently stretching the trim so that it lies smoothly and evenly along the stitching area. If using pins, be sure to remove the pins before they reach the cutting blades. Or baste the trim in place first using a sewing machine.

Seam Stabilization

Trims are also used to provide stabilization to knitted seams, particularly shoulder seams. There are 2 types of trim used: stay tapes and elastic. For seams that need to be strong and stable without stretching, a woven stay tape is serged into the seam as it is stitched.

If the seam needs to be able to stretch, a thin elastic, such as clear elastic, is used instead. This is especially effective for sportswear applications.

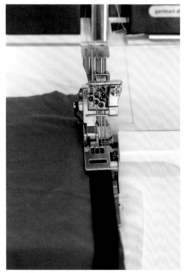

Serging stay tape onto a seam

FLAT CONSTRUCTION METHOD FOR KNITWEAR

The fashion industry created the flat construction method to take advantage of serger stitching speed and make the process more efficient than traditional clothing construction methods.

The goal of flat construction is to streamline the construction process and to work with the garment pieces lying flat as much as possible, which is faster and easier than working in the round. This method can be applied to nearly any garment, but is especially effective when sewing basic knit T-shirts, sweatshirts, and other knit garments, including pants.

To Flatten Or Not To Flatten?

While the flat construction method is the fastest way to put a garment together, it is not the most attractive. Higher quality knit garments do not use the flat method to attach collars and hems, choosing instead to sew these details in a more conventional manner. Set-in sleeves are also more attractive and less bulky than a sleeve and seam sewn all-in-one. It is possible to use a combination of flat construction and traditional construction techniques while constructing a garment. Let your personal taste and preferences guide your serging construction choices.

Sergers are wonderful for creating much more than just knitwear. Sergers are fantastic for projects made with woven fabrics as well. They make quick work of taming fraying seam allowances and speed up construction by eliminating the need for separate seam finishes. Regardless of fabric type, serging is the fastest way to sew.

CHOOSING A COMPATIBLE STITCH

Choosing the most compatible serger stitches for a woven project is similar to choosing for knits. Strength and sometimes stretchability must be taken into consideration. In addition, woven fabrics fray.

Tip // Woven Stitch Chart
Use the handy woven stitch chart (page 68) to help choose the best stitch for your fabric.

Most serger stitches meet all of these woven compatibility requirements quite easily. So deciding which serger stitch to use is often based on seam attractiveness. Serger seam bulk can be an issue with garment sewing compatibility.

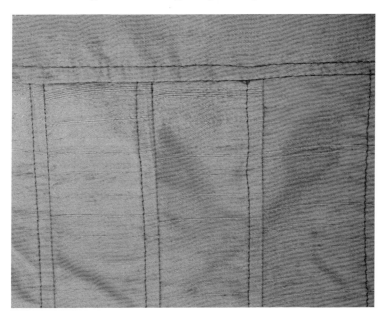

A serged seam, with both pieces of fabric sewn together into one seam allowance, is bulkier than a traditional sewn seam where the individual seam allowances are pressed open. For this reason, serged overlock seams are not always attractive in a woven garment. But flatlocking and narrow satin-stitched seams created with the rolled hem stitch can be used for alternative seaming methods.

Tip // Flatlock for Wovens
Flatlock stitches aren't just for knits! Use them to create attractive seams or topstitching details for wovens.

Bulk Can Be Beautiful

Turn serger seam bulk into an asset by using it to highlight seam construction details.

Woven garment with prominent seam even without topstitching

Press seam allowances to one side, then topstitch in place on the right side to create a faux welt seam.

Serged seam with topstitching

WOVEN CONSTRUCTION TECHNIQUES

Interpreting Garment Patterns For Serging

Patterns are rarely written with explicit serger instructions. But most garments can be successfully constructed with a serger. For easiest serging, look for patterns with simple design lines. Unlined garments are usually the simplest and look attractive with serger seaming. More complex garments with details such as notched collars, welt pockets, and buttonholes will require some portions to be sewn with a traditional sewing machine.

Serging Seam Allowances

Sergers are often used to finish the seam allowances on woven fabrics, even if the seam itself will be sewn with a traditional sewing machine. Using an overlock stitch keeps seam allowances from fraying and provides an attractive finish that mimics ready-to-wear clothing.

Tip // Whisker-Free Zone
Serging woven seam allowances is a great way to remove frayed fibers from the edge of the seam.

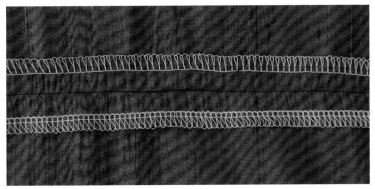
Serged seam allowances

When serging seam allowances before garment construction, the edge of the fabric must skim along the cutting blade without being cut. Ideally, the cutting blade should only remove any long "whiskers" from the edge of the fabric.

Trimming off fabric whiskers

If the serger cuts into the fabric it changes the seam allowance, making it difficult to fit and sew an accurate seam. Practice serging along the edge of scrap fabrics to perfect this skill.

Tip // Practical Skill Building
Create cleaning cloths from old towels and t-shirts by cutting the fabric into squares and serging around the edges. It's a great way to practice finishing seam allowances.

Seaming Accurately with a Serger

If a serger is used for seam construction, it is essential that the seam allowances are sewn accurately. The width of the serger seam varies depending on what stitch is chosen. The different needle positions combined with the action of the cutting blade make marking and sewing an accurate seam less obvious than on a traditional sewing machine.

Marked seam allowance set against foot needle marks

MARKING SEAM ALLOWANCES

The key to sewing accurately is using a stitching guide based on your seam allowance.

Tip // Creating a Stitching Guide
Learn more about how to create a serger stitching guide (page 73).

If there are no usable marks, you can easily create your own with a piece of removable tape.

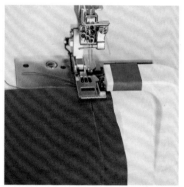

Blue tape placed in alignment with fabric edge

This will give you a visual reference to keep your seam allowance accurate when stitching. If there are needle alignment marks on your serger presser foot, check which mark aligns with the needle to the furthest left.

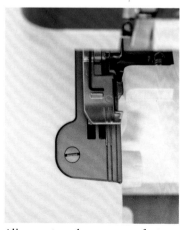

Alignment marks on presser foot

Serged seams are difficult to alter once sewn. A serged item can be made smaller, but not larger. Woven fabrics are less forgiving than knits, making it even more important to be sure your stitching lines are accurate and that the garment or item will fit.

Basted seam

Tip // Always Fit First
Fit and baste garment seams *before* serging for best results.

For the best guarantee of fitting and serging success, baste the seams first using a traditional sewing machine. Once the fit has been confirmed, simply leave the basting stitches in place and align them with the needle alignment mark on the serger presser foot as a secondary stitching guide. This is especially helpful when inserting a set-in sleeve, or serging slippery fabrics.

Tip // Sew Twice, Cut Once
It may seem counterproductive to sew the seams twice—once by sewing machine, and once by serger. But stitch basting can save time, money, and frustration by ensuring a successful garment.

Differential Feed for Wovens

Wovens may be more stable than knits, but they still benefit from adjusting the differential feed. If the seam appears to be puckering, slow down (reduce) the differential feed to help keep the fabric taut while serging. Speed up the differential feed (increase) to help ease in sleeve caps.

Easing sleeve cap with serger

Tip // Fancy Footwork
Use differential feed for creating special effects like ruffles, which are especially easy to do if using a gathering foot (page 135).

Specialty Techniques and Tools

and Delicates

Sergers are fabulous for working with sheers and other delicate fabrics. Sergers can create quick and attractive alternatives to traditional seaming and hemming methods that make even these tricky textiles a joy to sew. Serging is perfect for creating lingerie, evening wear, or specialty home decor.

CHOOSING A COMPATIBLE STITCH

Delicate and sheer fabrics have very simple serging requirements. The seam must be attractive, and not bulky. For this reason, it is best to use narrow 2- or 3-thread stitches to seam and hem these special fabrics. Use the seaming strength considerations as the criteria when deciding between 2- or 3-thread stitches. A 2-thread stitch is lighter weight, but 3-thread is stronger. Choose lightweight threads in both the needle and loopers, and fine, sharp needles for best results.

PREPARING DELICATE FABRICS

Fabric preparation ensures success when serging sheers and delicates. If the fabric is hand-washable, a liquid fabric stabilizer such as spray starch, PerfectSew, or Terial Magic can make cutting and serging much easier. Pretreat the entire fabric yardage before cutting and leave the stabilizer in the fabric throughout the construction process.

Pretreated chiffon

Stiffen For Success

Delicate and sheer fabrics benefit from the extra support given by stiffening the fabric with a liquid stabilizer or starch. Even if the fabric is already stiff, it likely has a loose weave structure that can be difficult to serge without the fabric falling apart at the seam or hem. Stiffening the fabric keeps the woven threads in place during cutting and construction.

To pre-treat your delicate fabric, follow these steps:

1. Prewash (by hand) a small test sample to check for shrinkage and dye stability. If it handwashes safely, continue to the next steps.

2. Place the fabric yardage in a large bowl or sink. If the starch/stabilizer is in a spray bottle, spray the fabric, being careful to turn the fabric so it is saturated evenly. If the stabilizer is a liquid, pour a small amount on the fabric and gently knead to distribute evenly. Gently squeeze out the excess liquid. Rolling the fabric in an old towel may also be necessary to remove the excess. The treated fabric should ideally be damp, not wet. Thick liquid stabilizers may need to be diluted. Check the product instructions before applying.

3. Lay the fabric flat on a washable table surface, or carefully hang on a drying rack. A shower curtain rod can also be used. Hang the fabric selvages as straight as possible and gently smooth out creases and wrinkles before allowing to dry.

4. Once dry, gently steam press any wrinkles and straighten the fabric if necessary.

5. Cut and serge the fabric as you normally would.

6. Once the project is completed, wash the liquid stabilizer out of the fabric. Use liquid fabric softener in the rinse water to restore the "hand", or original feel of the fabric. Air dry the project until nearly dry. A gentle tumble in the dryer on low or no (air dry) heat helps to completely re-soften the finished project.

BEAUTIFUL SERGER CONSTRUCTION

Serger seams may be practical, but they can also be pretty. There are several seaming and hemming techniques that are particularly suitable for serging delicate fabrics. Always stitch test samples for appearance and compatibility before serging your project.

Mock French Seams

Seams for sheers can be seen through the fabric, so they must be attractive. Sergers can create a seam that looks like a traditional French seam from the outside, but in a fraction of the time. Use a 2- or 3-thread narrow overlock for a beautiful small seam.

Tip // Stop the Slippage
If you have difficulty with the yarns of the fabric weave slipping (pulling apart) along the seam, use a wide overlock setting instead of narrow.

Mock French seam

Flatlocked Lace

Creating fancy lace edging perfect for lingerie is fast and easy using a flatlock stitch. Simply align the edge of the lace with the fabric edge, right sides together.

Flatlock using a narrow flatlock stitch along the edge of the fabric and lace, being careful not to cut into the lace border. Disengage the cutting blade if necessary.

Once flatlocked, gently pull the lace edging flat and press.

Tip // Easy Lace Alignment
Many sergers have an optional lace/hem foot that aligns lace and fabric edges for easy flat-locking.

Satin-Stitched Seams

Decorative satin-stitched narrow seams are perfect for seaming sheer fabrics.

Satin-stitched seam created with rolled hem

To create this beautiful effect, set up your serger for a 3-thread rolled hem. Insert 2 pieces of scrap fabric and test the stitch, adjusting the stitch length and cutting depth if necessary. Also test for seam allowance alignment and mark accordingly.

Serge the seams using the adjusted rolled hem stitch. Use a thread sealant to secure the thread chains and trim close to the fabric when dry.

ROLLED HEM TIPS

Rolled hems make a wonderful finish for delicate fabrics. But chiffon and other loosely woven fabrics can be shifty and difficult to hem. Follow one or all of these tips for easier rolled hem success with challenging fabrics.

1. Starch or pre-stabilize the fabric edge. This helps the weave structure stay intact.

2. If the hem is slipping off the edge of the fabric, try increasing the cutting width to bring more fabric into the hem.

3. Decrease (shorten) stitch length to wrap the fabric more closely.

4. Place 1″-wide strips of wash-away stabilizer under the fabric edge as you serge. It will help the fabric edge to roll smoothly, be caught securely, and minimize whiskers.

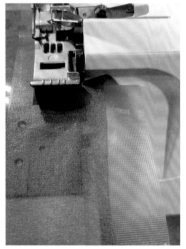

Place wash-away stabilizer under fabric edge.

Photo by Katrina Walker

CHAPTER 11

Specialty Tools

Many sergers have optional accessory feet that are available to create decorative effects or make specialty serging techniques easier to sew. The number and type of feet available vary by brand and model. Consult your serger manual to learn which accessory feet are available for your serger.

OVERLOCK FEET

These specialty feet are designed to work with the serger's overlock or rolled hem stitches. Some are used for construction, but many of them produce beautiful embellishments that are unique to the serger.

Beading Foot

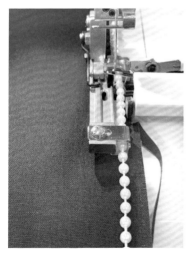 

Photo by Katrina Walker

The beading foot guides pre-strung beads, pearls, or similar for attaching along the edge of hems. This can be used to create beautiful bridal veils, scarves, and other accessories.

Blindhem/Lace Foot

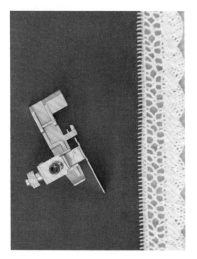

Photo by Katrina Walker

The blindhem foot is sometimes also used as a lace attaching foot. It aligns the fold of a blind hem to the edge of lace so that a flatlock stitch creates an attractive hem or edging.

Corded/Yarn Edge Foot

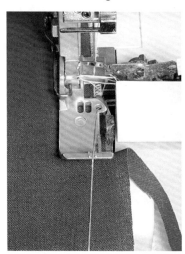
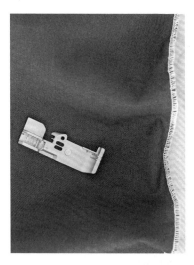

Photo by Katrina Walker

The corded/yarn edge foot guides cording or yarn into a rolled hem. It's often used with stiff monofilament to create a wavy decorative hem.

Elastic Foot

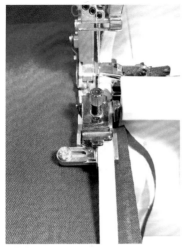
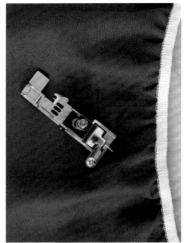

Photo by Katrina Walker

The elastic foot guides and pre-stretches elastic as it is serged in 1 application. The amount of stretch can usually be varied with an adjustment screw and by using the differential feed.

Gathering Foot

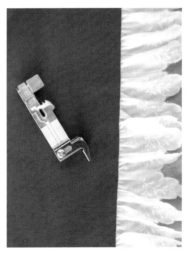

Photo by Katrina Walker

The gathering foot uses a separator plate so that 1 layer of fabric can be gathered using the differential feed, while simultaneously attaching the gathered fabric to a second piece of flat fabric.

Piping Foot

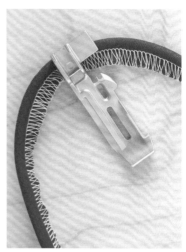

Photo by Katrina Walker

The piping foot allows premade piping to be inserted into a seam accurately while serging. It also allows piping to be created.

Taping Foot

Photo by Katrina Walker

The taping foot applies seam tape to seams while stitching. This reinforces and stabilizes seams for shoulders and other areas.

COVERLOCK FEET

These specialty feet are designed to work specifically with the coverstitch or chain stitch. Some are similar in function to overlock feet, but many are unique to the capabilities of the coverlock machine.

Binding Foot

Photo by Katrina Walker

The binding foot folds and aligns lightweight binding so it can be attached in 1 operation.

Clear Coverstitch Foot

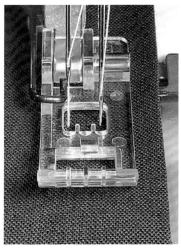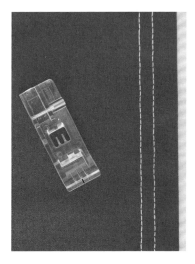

Photo by Katrina Walker

The clear coverstitch foot is made of clear plastic making it easier to see and stitch accurately while coverstitching.

Belt Loop and Strap Foot

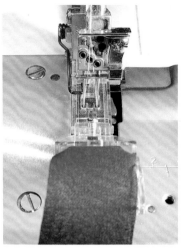
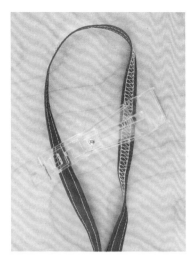

Photo by Katrina Walker

The belt loop and strap foot uses a folding flange on the front to create coverstitched belt loops in one operation.

Fold and Join Trim Foot

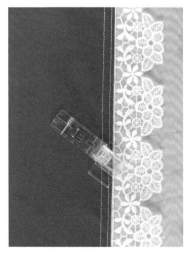

Photo by Katrina Walker

The fold and join trim foot guides hem edges into place, and a secondary guide aligns trim for attachment with a coverstitch.

Piping Foot

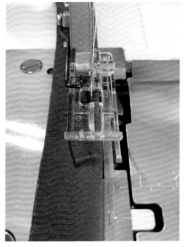
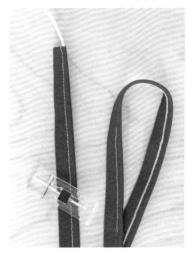

Photo by Katrina Walker

The coverstitch piping foot creates piping using the chain stitch. It can also create corded tucks using the coverstitch.

Trim Foot

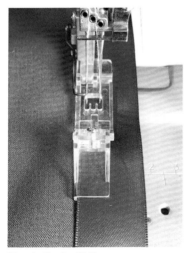

Photo by Katrina Walker

The trim foot aligns lace and other decorative trims for coverstitching into place.

Index

2

2-thread converter..............14, 31

2-thread flatlock 57, 67–69, 89

2-thread narrow edge ... 57, 67–68

2-thread overlock ... 52, 56–57, 67–69

2-thread rolled hem ... 59, 62, 67–68, 95

2-thread stitches 56

2-thread wrapped overlock 58, 67–69

3

3-thread flatlock 52, 57, 60–61, 67–69, 89

3-thread narrow edge ... 60, 68–69

3-thread overlock 34, 36, 52, 59–60, 67–69, 101, 113

3-thread rolled hem 62, 67–69, 95–96, 131

3-thread stitches 14, 59, 128

3-thread stretch overlock ...62, 67

3-thread wrapped overlock 61, 67–69

4

4-thread overlock ... 14–15, 34, 36, 53, 62–63, 67–69, 76, 113

4-thread safety stitch 63–64, 68–69, 72

4-thread stitches 56, 62

5

5-thread safety stitch 53, 64, 68–69, 100–103, 109

5-thread stitches 64

A

accessory box 22

air threading...... 12–13, 26, 28–29

air threading ports 12

Allen wrench 22

B

backstitching 49, 107

basting ... 10, 56, 68–69, 74–75, 93, 115, 125

basting serger seams 74

beading foot 133

belt loop foot 138

belt loops 10, 16, 138

binding foot 137

blind hem 91, 134

blindhem foot 134

C

chaining off 81–82

chain stitch... 10, 13, 39–45, 48, 53, 56, 68–69, 72, 100–102, 137, 139

clear coverstitch foot 137

color-coded threading ...26, 29–30, 32, 40

corded edge foot 134

coverlock feet 133, 137

coverstitching 34, 39, 49, 100–109, 137

cutting blade adjustment knob ...19

cutting blades ... 17, 19–20, 23, 52, 55, 60, 72–74, 76, 78–83, 90–91, 96, 99, 103–104, 118, 123–124, 131

D

decorative threads ...25, 51, 90, 96

differential feed ... 18, 71, 75–76, 94, 97–98, 111, 114, 125, 135

double-ended needle 22

E

elastic foot 135

F

feed dogs 16–18, 75

fit 75, 115, 123, 125

flat construction 117, 119

flatlock ...52, 57–58, 60–61, 67–69, 74, 88–93, 121, 131, 134

fold and join trim foot 138

foot control 21, 38, 77

fray inhibitor 23

fusible web 106

G

garment patterns 122

gathering foot 125, 135

H

handwheel ... 16, 26, 31, 37, 38, 40, 82, 102

hems ...24, 39, 51, 58, 63–64, 67–69, 91, 94–99, 104–106, 116, 119, 132

K

knit construction 111–119

knit stitch chart 112

L

lace foot 134

lettuce-edge hem 76, 94, 97–98

lint brush 23

liquid stabilizer.............. 128–130

looper, chain-stitch ...13, 39–41, 53, 55–56, 63, 100–101, 104, 109

looper, lower..... 13, 27–28, 31–33, 38–41, 52–53, 55–56, 59, 89, 95, 99, 109

looper threader 23

looper, upper ... 13–14, 27, 29–33, 38, 52–53, 55–56, 89, 95, 99, 109

M

marking cutting line 78

marking seam allowance ... 71–74

mock blanket stitch 92

mock French seams 130

N

napkins 96

needle bar 34, 36, 42, 44, 48

needle clamp 14

needles 12, 14–18, 26, 28, 34, 36–42, 44, 48–49, 54, 55, 62, 74, 78, 82–84, 89, 92, 95, 99, 101, 103–109, 128

needle threader 23

P

PerfectSew 128

pinning 74

piping foot 136

precutting......................... 78, 81

presser foot... 16–17, 27, 30, 72–77, 124–125

presser foot pressure adjustment 17

pretreating fabric..................128

pull-through method...............50

Q

quartering 116–118

R

removable tape 73, 105, 124

rethreading 38

ribbon insertion 90

rolled hem 55, 59, 62, 67–69, 95–99, 114, 121, 131–134

S

safety overlock........................27

satin-stitched seams....... 121, 131

scarf................................. 95–96

screen interface 20

screwdriver 23

seam allowance 19, 24, 71–74, 76, 78, 80–81, 83–84, 113, 115, 121–124, 131

seam guide 73–74, 76, 105, 124

seam ripping 66

seam slippage 130

seam stabilization 118

securing serger chain 82, 85

selecting serger stitches ... 67–69, 89

serger basic parts 10

serger buying tips 24

serger feet 16, 24, 105, 133–139

serger foot alignment marks ... 73, 124

serger reference notebook ... 55, 69

serger threading diagram ... 26, 29, 32, 40

serger yarn 25, 96, 134

serging a circle 78, 81

serging corners 81–85

serging curves 78–81

serging knits 111–119

serging wovens 120–125

sewing machine 9–11, 75, 115, 118, 122, 125

sewing machine oil 23

sheer fabrics 68, 127–132

specialty feet 16, 24, 133–139

specialty trims 116

speed adjustment 21

speed control 21, 78

spray starch 99, 113, 128

stabilizer 92, 104–106, 108–109, 113, 128–130, 132

stay tape 118

stitch chart 55, 67–69, 112

stitch finger 18, 27, 55, 95

stitching guide ... 73, 115, 124–125

stitch plate 17–18, 30, 32–33, 37, 41, 55, 95

stitch reference chart ... 67–69, 112

stitch selection 20

strap foot 138

stretch testing 112–113

T

taping foot 136

tension discs ... 11–12, 14, 20, 27, 29, 32, 35–36, 40, 43–44, 46–47, 51

tension setting ... 55, 69, 89, 95, 99, 101, 104

Terial Magic 128

thread chain 37–38, 76–77, 82, 85–86

thread cone holder 23

thread cone rack 11

thread guides 11–12, 29–30, 32, 35, 40, 43

threading 11–13, 16, 23, 25–53, 109

threading lever 13, 33, 41

threading mode 26

thread nets 23

thread sealant 51, 77, 86, 131

thread snips 23

thread tension 26–27, 29, 49, 52–53, 93, 109

thread unreeling discs 23

topstitching 56, 88, 90, 104, 121–122

trim foot 138–139

troubleshooting ... 52, 93, 98, 103, 109

T-shirts 119

tweezers 23, 30, 33, 41

V

vacuum attachment 23

W

waste catcher 23

whiskers 99, 123, 132

Wonder Clips 74

woven construction 120–125

woven stitch chart 68–69

Y

yarn edge foot 134